Intriguing Wiltshire

K.G. JONES

HALSGROVE

First published in Great Britain in 2016

British Library Cataloguing-in-Publication Data
A CIP record for this title is available from the British Library

ISBN 978 0 85704 286 6

HALSGROVE
Halsgrove House,
Ryelands Business Park,
Bagley Road, Wellington, Somerset TA21 9PZ
Tel: 01823 653777   Fax: 01823 216796
email: sales@halsgrove.com

Part of the Halsgrove group of companies
Information on all Halsgrove titles is available at: www.halsgrove.com

Printed and bound in China by Everbest Printing Investment Ltd

Contents

Acknowledgements

My thanks go to, in the first instance, my wife, Elizabeth, for proof reading as the work progressed and correcting grammatical errors and for extra research where information has been difficult to obtain. Also to Allannah Daniel for proof reading the finished work. Research and photography has taken a very long time to complete with many miles of motoring. Following this many hours of word processing and photoshop work, which has taken me away from the comfort of the living room and the company of my wife, which makes her a treasure for putting up with it!

A big thank you to all the artists and sculptors who have allowed their work to be placed in the public domain. Special thanks to Richard Cowdy and Gordon Dickenson for information on their sculpting work; Joanna Dewfall (www.dewfallmosaic.co.uk) for help with understanding the creation of mosaic panels; Darryl Moody, local studies, Swindon Central Library; the Swindon and Wiltshire History Centre; Chatsworth House for information on the Walking Madonna; Adrian Green and Louise Tunnard, Salisbury Museum; Andrew Lunt church warden at Little Langford; Val Edwards, Artsite in Swindon; the Tourist Information Offices throughout the county for their help with maps to locate my quarry; the Salisbury Civic Society; the Salisbury Arts Centre and last but not least, the Wiltshire Museum in Devizes.

Then there are friends and family who have helped with specialised and local information; the late Norman Chant, Elizabeth's father, who trawled through many articles and books to find items of interest, Mary and David Cracknell, my son Stephen Jones, Erik Neale, Jack Rudd and Ben Underwood.

Finally all those people in passing from whom I have sought information on local matters and those that have pointed me in the direction of things of interest that were close at hand yet I was unaware existed.

Preface

When I was a child my mother taught me about flora and fauna and things to see while out and about, all those intriguing things other people pass by. In other words she encouraged me to be observant. During school days my observations turned to transport, particularly railways (still a favourite pastime when steam engines are about). I remember thinking about the journeys made by the locomotives and their rake of carriages on the final leg of their journey into Paddington. What countryside had they passed through, what had the passengers seen through the windows and had they passed the Great Western Railway Works in Swindon? Then there were the Sunday double decker bus tours from Uxbridge in Middlesex around London seeing the sights from the front seats on the top deck, providing you were first on the bus!

Firmly implanted in my memory were the school days out at the end of term, during my education at Slough Grammar School. Where were we going to travel to and what would we see? About a week before the travel days (obviously meant to further educate us!) a list would be given to each child requesting the parents contribution to the coach hire. I don't remember it being expensive and I was never held back from travelling. However, I don't know whether my parents ever went without to let me go.

On one of the lists were St Alban's Cathedral and the City Roman remains and on another day, Old Sarum, Salisbury and Stonehenge. Both of these trips were ideal opportunities to search for relics of the past, for a youthful ambition was to find an artefact, a piece of worked flint or a fragment from an old castle, just lying on the ground waiting to be picked up. Needless to say I never found anything, but I remember it being fun looking. Ironically I have since found numerous pieces of worked Mesolithic flint whilst digging our Wiltshire garden.

However, it was Wiltshire that fascinated me, the undulating plain, the Neolithic long barrows and round tumuli of the Bronze age, Iron Age hill forts, the old buildings of Salisbury and above all, Stonehenge. Little did I know in those far off days that at a future date I would be living in my favourite county within twenty minutes of the world's most famous circle and only ten minutes from the tallest spire in the British Isles. I hope I qualify to be a Moonraker, having lived within sight of Salisbury Cathedral spire for almost fifteen years, despite not being born in the county.

It was natural that having been taught to be watchful at an early age that I became interested in photography. My first attempts at recording objects and wildlife soon proved to me that I had the wrong camera – a box with no adjustments and no quality either, it just wouldn't do. What would I like for Christmas? You guessed it – a camera that works please. From the day I was given my first 35mm camera and a colour slide film, I have been hardly anywhere without a camera to record my observations. I joined a camera club (more teaching to be observant). I learnt about composition, depth of field, exposure and how to process film.

Of course film has now practically been replaced with digital imaging. At first reluctant to use the medium, I am now solely working digitally, including using computer technology and software to produce good quality images that improve with every new higher megapixel count camera that I purchase. I am now extremely happy with the quality I achieve and feel any further improvement with technology and file sizes will fill my hard drive unnecessarily.

Tucked away in a container with a silica gel bag to prevent corrosion, I have kept all my film cameras for nostalgic purposes and all my important film negatives and slides for posterity. However, all the digital photographs that we now take and keep in computer files could easily be wiped from the memories of devices and lost for ever. At the moment I can see a generation of family and topographical photographs lost to the future, unless printed copies are made and personally archived.

Since moving near Salisbury I became interested in the photography of Wiltshire public works of art, waymarkers, urban and rural features through time and indeed time itself, significant commemorations and memorials, past county transport and communications and a miscellany of everything else of passing interest. Put all these features together and *Intriguing Wiltshire* has come to fruition. There is far too much for a single volume, so much will depend how this volume is received whether there is more to follow.

Almost everything included in *Intriguing Wiltshire* series is free to see, with one or two exceptions necessary to complete a theme. For this reason some well known county properties are excluded, owned by the National Trust or privately, which will also exclude some works of art, purely because they are not in the free public domain.

The area covered is within the boundary of Wiltshire and Swindon. It has taken many years to discover, photograph and research each individual subject. I must apologise for any significant theme omissions, which I am sure there must be, bearing in mind the extent of this work and the size of Wiltshire. One cannot expect to view all of my subject matter from a car window, but by all means use the vehicle to reach a suitable car parking space, then walk as a wayfarer to use your powers of observation and discover the myriad of interest on a wide range of subject matter that abides in moonraking country.

K.G. Jones
Alderbury, Wiltshire, 2016

Introduction

This volume of *Intriguing Wiltshire*, has taken many years to compile. Not because the length of time in preparation or the taking of photographs has been excessive, but the actual discovery of all that there is to see, then photograph. This has often meant returning to the same location to view, record and photograph subjects of which I had been unaware. There are many books written covering different aspects of Wiltshire and there are snippets of information in all of them, which are starting points for further investigation. I have also found the internet a wonderful tool of discovery and research, as long as one knows what to look for. Even so, having covered most places in the county on foot, having reached each destination by car or public transport, there is a probability that I have missed items of the subject themes covered by this book that are worthy of inclusion. I have tried to double check all the facts, but apologise for any errors that may come to light, as I do not profess to be a master of all the diverse subjects covered.

So what inspiration has spurred me on to put pen to paper and share my discoveries with others. I have already mentioned in the preface how it all began, with encouragement from my mother, who had a love of the countryside and all that it contained. I have a small library of books related to county topography and since moving to Wiltshire, many on the subject of Wessex in which Wiltshire is situated and of the county itself. By the nature of topography some are in the form of gazetteers. Among these are two books which inspired me on the trail of discovery with my camera: Arthur Mee's *The Kings England – Wiltshire* and the *Shell Guide to Wiltshire*. The latter is full of monochrome photography and whilst black and white has its place, I considered how much improved the subject matter would be in colour. Furthermore, whilst the original photography would have been of a high standard, often the old printing processes leave the illustrations dark and muddy.

So with colour and quality in mind, this volume covers a wide range of topics, concentrating to a lesser extent on buildings and landscape features, which are saved for another day, but more on subjects of interest found by the wayside and close to hand in town and country. The main theme running through the book is an A to Z Gazetteer of places within the county (which includes Swindon) and the appealing subject matter discovered at each location. This includes, as principal topics, Public Works of Art and Civil Commemorations, which I have tried to cover comprehensively. However, there are other items of miscellaneous nature, which will, hopefully fascinate the reader.

Throughout the Gazetteer are regular interludes to change the mood. I have called these Spotlights, which cover a wide subject matter from Roadside Furniture to Inn and Pub Signs, and other diverse topics such as Saxon Crosses, Window Tax and White Horses.

Returning to one of the feature topics of the Gazetteer: Public Works of Art. The Swindon area has a large amount of public art, in wall murals, sculpture and pavement mosaic. There is also, unfortunately, a degree of bad graffiti on walls, some of which once had murals. The old and new town and the wider outskirts cover a large area and it has taken seven visits to find everything discovered in books, on the internet and with my own encounters. Much of the art in Swindon has been funded under the Percent for Art scheme, where public money is matched with developers' contributions.

A mosaic in Castlefields in Calne on a nature theme.

Even with the wealth of written and recorded information available, I have turned a corner in a town street to find a sculpture or piece of artwork that had only recently been placed there. Herein lies the problem of trying to be comprehensive! For example the Salisbury Market Square is a large open space in the centre of the

Sculptures at Heavens Gate.

city. I am aware that an item of public art is due to be placed there, but never seems to materialise. There is a law of inconvenience that will place it as soon as I am unable to include it. The law has a name, which I will refrain from mentioning!

During my research and travels through Wiltshire I have found that some of the more significant commemorations are related to the Golden and Diamond Jubilees of Queen Victoria and Queen Elizabeth II. The new Millennium was also an excuse for habitations to select a Wiltshire sarsen stone from the downs and have a plaque engraved to celebrate the year 2000.

The location of each subject in the Gazetteer is provided with an ordnance survey grid reference to three figures, which approximates its position. Studying large scale maps of the county and compiling *Intriguing Wiltshire* has given me a great deal of pleasure, as well as greatly expanding the knowledge of my home county. If the reader doesn't live in Wiltshire, by turning these pages and visiting some of the places, I am sure you will become an adopted Moonraker and return time and time again. Take care during your travels and enjoy walking in my footsteps.

Spotlight on Boundaries

Wiltshire including the Borough of Swindon is a county of 1346 square miles (3485 square kilometres). It borders Gloucestershire and Oxfordshire in the north, Berkshire and Hampshire in the east, Dorset in the south and Somerset in the west. Its county town is Trowbridge, but prior to 1930 was Wilton. In the ninth century, in Saxon Wessex, the area was known as Wiltunscir. In present day Wiltshire there are 21 towns and Salisbury city.

The county is characterised by Salisbury Plain, an area of undulating downland, which since the First World War has had a military presence as a training ground. Within the downland is the iconic landmark of Stonehenge. To the south of the plain, in the Avon Valley, is Salisbury Cathedral and in the north Cotswold Country is encountered. There is a rich heritage of prehistory with Stone, Bronze and Iron Ages well represented.

Traditional Wiltshire County Boundaries

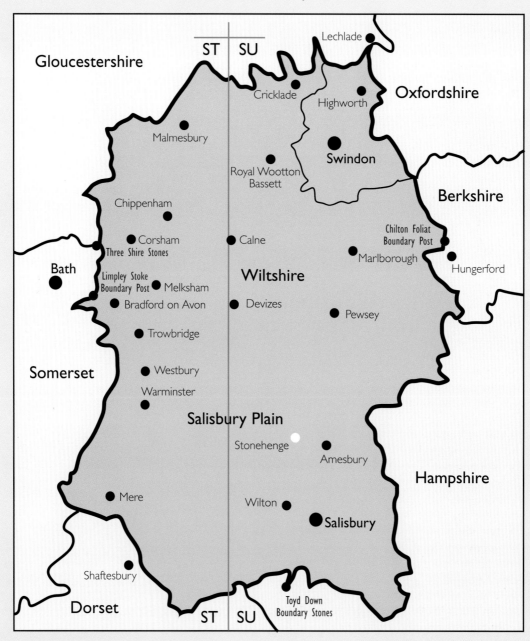

Clockwise from top left: *1. The county boundary for Wiltshire is on all main highways entering the county. 2. The boundary between Wiltshire and Hampshire is marked with stone at Toyd Down (SU 089 206). 3. On the shorter of the two stones is a crown a letter S and a date of 1891. 4. The Three Shire Stones mark the historic border between Somerset, Wiltshire and Gloucestershire (ST 796 701). 5. The boundary marker between Wiltshire and Berkshire near Chilton Foliat (SU 327 703). 6. The county boundary between Somerset and Wiltshire is on the Limpley Stoke viaduct on the A36 (ST 781 620).*

The main lines of the old Great Western Railway run east - west through the north and centre of the county and the old Southern Railway runs through the south of the county, with a connection south to north via Westbury. Prior to the railways, canals carried most of the heavy goods through the county. The principal roads run through the county from London to the West of England and Bristol and from the south coast to Bristol and the north of the county and beyond. The main artery through the Wiltshire is the M4 to South Wales.

At this point I welcome you to Wiltshire, as the green boundary sign does when entering the county on its major roads. An adjacent county boundary sign is often spaced a short distance away on the opposite side of the road, leaving a short stretch of "No man's land" in between. I suppose the actual boundary is the centre line between the two signs – not that it matters greatly, except if you live between the two!

The manner of marking the actual boundary between two counties varies greatly depending on the location. Frequently a significant change of direction in the boundary, as on Toyd Down is just marked with a stone (in this case two stones). The boundary marker

between Wiltshire and Berkshire is a cast iron post. The same design of post appears separating Hampshire and Berkshire, so I must conclude that Berkshire was responsible for marking the boundary.

Perhaps the most unusual boundary marker in England is the Three Shire Stones marker, situated on the Fosse Way near Colerne. Although taking on the appearance of a cromlech from prehistoric times, the Three Shire Stones are in fact a folly erected in 1859 at

One of three original 1736– dated Shire Stones beside the Fosse Way.

the meeting point of the boundaries of the historic counties of Gloucestershire, Somerset and Wiltshire.

The tripoint stones are set to the west side of the Fosse Way, the Roman road between Exeter and Lincoln. Inside the upright stones are the original tripoint stones in place since 1736. Each of the stones has a county initial, (G, S and W) together with an inscribed date of 1736. The folly stones over the originals are possibly from a burial chamber close to the site.

Parish boundaries within Wiltshire are frequently unmarked, but a number of cast iron examples are found on the A36 (on the old road through villages now by-passed). Simple boundary stones may be used in other cases. In recent years more care has been taken of these bygone relics of roadside furniture and they have been cleaned and repainted.

Tiddleywink (ST 872 758).

Situated on the old A36 west of Steeple Langford (SU 030 378). The "T" may represent Turnpike.

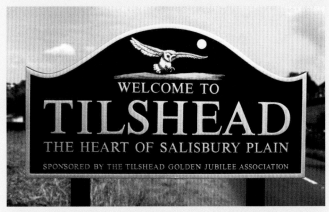

Tilshead in the middle of Salisbury Plain (SU 028 479).

The boundary marker between Alderbury and Laverstock situated on the old A36 near the Downton turn (SU 174 281).

To let travellers know that they are entering the bounds of a village or town a sign placed on the boundary advertises the fact. Such a sign will be placed on all principal roads into the settlement. The better signs have pictorial information about the community being entered, often a principal feature and are cast in metal with relief wording and artwork. Painted or printed signs do not have longevity and fade or flake and periodically require replacing , but can be very appealing when they are fresh.

The most amusing name for a Wiltshire hamlet is "Tiddleywink." I certainly raised a smile when I first encountered it, stopped and photographed it. It is an

Shrewton shows its lock up on the sign (SU 075 432).

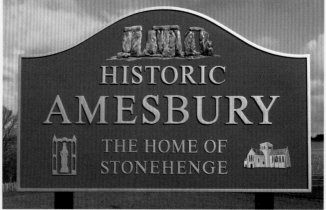

Left from top:
1. The village sign for Alderbury and
Whaddon situated between the two. Among the features on
the sign are brickmaking, the green Dragon public house and
the Three Crowns public house (SU 192 268).
2. The artwork of Easterton village sign (SU 021 549).
3. The A36 entrance to Salisbury in spring. (SU 158 291).

Above from top:
1. An attractive recent sign for the boundary
of Amesbury showing Stonehenge (SU 157 396).
2. The village of Keevil shows its connection with gliders and
Hercules aircraft used for training drops (ST 914 584).
3. A modern depiction of the down above Liddington
(SU 200 818).

area in Yatton Keynell and has carried the name since the 1870s, but not at the roadside and probably known only to the locals. It was first mentioned on the 1881 census return in Chippenham Road. The name is believed to have originated from an unlicensed beer house. It is a hamlet of eight houses and made news in 2003 when Wiltshire County Council decided to put road signs at either end of the hamlet to slow traffic down.

Canals and railways have boundaries, but markers are hard to find. There is a Kennet and Avon Canal marker at Avoncliff and there are, no doubt, others to seek out. The Great Western Railway had cast iron roundels, which are usually dated, but again difficult to find.

In North Meadow in Cricklade there are a number of boundary stones with initials of the owners of rights engraved on them. They date to 1824 after the enclosure award demarcated hay rights in the common field. The Cricklade site has 29 such boundary stones. Sometimes a boundary stone can be found without a clue as to its purpose and one has then to question whether or not it is on a boundary. One such example exists above Harnham on a footpath verge. It has a letter "A" engraved on one face with a date of 1753 below. The oddest boundary is that off a "Quiet Lane." There are a number of lanes meeting this criteria near Woodborough. There is very little traffic, virtually no habitation and one wonders why the obvious has to be stated.

Far left: *The Kennett and Avon marker on the verge of the canal at Avoncliff, near the aqueduct. It is possible this stone could just be an identification marker as it is probably away from the exact boundary fence.*

Left: *A mystery marker dated 1753 above Harnham on a footpath (SU 135 287).*

Far left: *One of a number of Quiet Lane signs guarding country lanes near Woodborough.*

Left: *One of the hay right markers in North Meadow Cricklade. The meadow is a nature reserve and in the spring has a host of fritillaries on display (typically SU 095 945).*

Detached Wiltshire

Prior to 1844 many counties had detached parts in other counties. Wiltshire, for example, had islands of land in Berkshire. These were some distance from the main county boundary of Wiltshire with Berkshire in the west. This rather odd arrangement was probably the result of the recording of Domesday estates and accidents of land ownership.

To add to the boundary irregularities, between Berkshire and Wiltshire, a finger of land in the south west corner of Berkshire stretched into Wiltshire, in which Shalbourne was situated. To the east of our county, villages now in Hampshire were once in Wiltshire and land has been exchanged between Wiltshire and Gloucestershire and Somerset.

The start of clearing this messy county border arrangement started in 1844 with the Counties Detached Parts Act. Thus the parts of Hurst, Shinfield and Wokingham that were detached islands of Wiltshire within Berkshire became part of Berkshire County.

Further boundary changes were made in by the Local Government Act of 1894, which transferred Shalbourne to Wiltshire and other boundary amendments with other counties.

Before moving to Wiltshire I lived in Berkshire not far from Hurst village. The village has Grade II listed almshouses with a plaque over the doorway, giving a commemoration of their foundation. The hospital (a term used at the time to describe almshouses) was founded in 1664 at the sole cost of William Barker of Hurst in the County of Wilts. He died in 1685 and is buried in the chancel of the parish church situated opposite the almshouses. The charity catered for eight poor persons each at 6d per diem for ever. I had for some time wondered what the reference to Wiltshire meant.

Above: *Within the pre-1844 Wiltshire island in Berkshire, Barker's Hospital was built in Hurst in 1664. The almshouses are situated in an attractive location opposite the parish church. In the photograph note the tandem tricycle, an unusual contraption, but probably safer and more stable than two wheels, except when cornering (SU 795 729).*

Left: *A cast iron boundary marker in Wokingham, with Wiltshire on the right and Berkshire on the left. (SU 815 688).*

Below: *The plaque above the entrance door to the almshouses provides evidence that Hurst was once in Wiltshire.*

Gazetteer

Aldbourne

Memorial to Rover (ST 265 756)

The village of Aldbourne has a memorial to a dog called Rover. It was erected by Aldbourne and Baydon parishioners in memory of the dog, who was a faithful worker for Savernake Hospital. The memorial was erected following the dog's death in 1933 after raising funds for the hospital since 1924.

It is unclear how the dog managed to raise money from the public, but I suspect it carried, over its back, a money box saddlebag in which the public posted their pennies. Such a charitable exercise was carried out on some large railway stations, where a dog with a money box patrolled the platforms raising cash for railway charities. Quite often the dog would be stuffed (after its demise!) and placed in a case on the platform in commemoration.

The breed of Rover is unknown, but I suspect it was a small mongrel with a docked tail, judging by the representation on the memorial. Aldbourne Archive would like to find a photograph of the dog, for their historical records.

Right: The remains of Ivychurch Priory in Alderbury c1910. The remains still exist today, but are private and not accessible to the public. The old postcard view serves to illustrate from whence the major components of the Fountain were obtained.

Alderbury

Fountain (SU 183 274)

Alderbury Fountain is situated on the village green. It commemorates the Coronation of Edward VII on 9 August 1902 and the provision of a water supply to the village by Jacob the sixth Earl of Radnor. A metal plaque describes the commemoration: "Erected by the parishioners of Alderbury in grateful acknowledgement of the great kindness and generosity of Jacob sixth Earl of Radnor in providing an abundant supply of water, and a commemoration of the Coronation of King Edward VII. August 9th 1902. Engineers. Merryweather and Sons, London."

A smaller plaque on the Fountain describes the origin of the Fountain's principal materials: "These columns and capitals are from the cloister of Ivychurch Priory. 12th century."

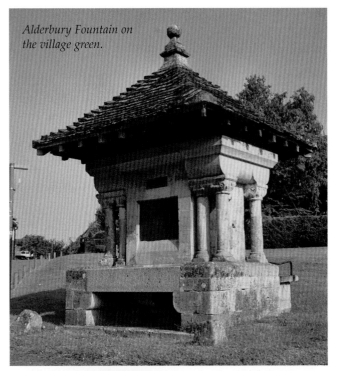

Alderbury Fountain on the village green.

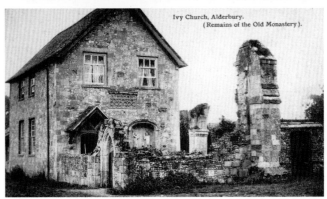

Ivy Church, Alderbury.
(Remains of the Old Monastery).

The history of Ivychurch Priory can be found in *More of the Mosaic of Alderbury and Whaddon* by the village history group. However, briefly, Ivychurch Priory was founded in 1139 by King Stephen. In 1534 Henry VIII divorced himself from Rome and became head of the Church of England. Two years later Ivychurch Priory was dissolved, in common with other monasteries and priories of the time. The property was in good repair and became a leased residence for most of its lifetime. In 1888 it was destroyed by fire.

Only a few remains are visible today incorporated into a farmhouse. There is no public access as the vestiges of the priory masonry are on private property.

With regard to the water supply, in 1902 Lord Radnor paid Messrs. Merryweather and Sons to pump water from a plentiful well at Longford Castle, Lord Radnor's residence, situated below Alderbury in the Avon Valley next to the river. The water was pumped to a reservoir above Ivychurch Farm. The head of water was adequate to supply both Longford Castle and Alderbury village via a water main and a number of standpipes.

Alderbury Fountain had water taps and a horse trough. The water taps have long disappeared.

Book Swap (SU 185 273)

Since the inception of the mobile phone age, giving everyone the choice of worldwide communication at their fingertips, the familiar red phone box is rapidly becoming redundant. How many today can remember putting money in the slot to build up talking time and pressing button A!

In Alderbury the phone box was unwanted and gathered cobwebs, so the Parish Council gave it a new lease of life and converted it into a Book Swap Library. The telephone and coin box have been removed and shelving added to contain the books, which everyone can access and remove a book to read. However, the library depends upon customers replacing each book taken with another that they have read. This, of course, relies upon trust, but when I photographed the Book Swap the shelves were full with popular reading. Thus the box's use has been changed from the spoken word to the written word, keeping the spirit of communication alive.

Alderbury phone box was becoming a home for spiders, before it was repainted and converted to a Book Swap Library.

All Cannings

Millenium Stone (SU 073 619)

A sarsen stone placed on the village green to commemorate the millennium. Part of the face of the stone has been polished and engraved with the wording: "All Cannings. 2000 AD. Population 649."

Arthur Mee in his *Kings England – Wiltshire* records that the poet Coleridge (1772 - 1834) was friendly with the rector Anthony Methuen. He stayed at the rectory for two years after the Battle of Waterloo (1815). It is unclear if the date of his stay has any significance in relation to the battle. The rectory is a listed building; the listing states that on an upper window is scratched: "Wi/Coleridge the poet. LJM 1809", indicating he possibly had an earlier stay at the rectory.

Alvediston

Sir Anthony Eden (ST 977 239)

Sir Anthony Eden, Earl of Avon (1897 - 1977) was a Prime Minister from April 1955, succeeding Winston Churchill, until his retirement due to ill health on 9 January 1957 – a short, but troubling time in office. He was created Earl of Avon in 1961 and lived in Manor House, Alvediston, from 1966 until his death in 1977. He is buried in St Mary's churchyard and there is a monument tablet with a low relief sculpture inside the church opposite the door. The sculptor was Martin Jennings.

Anthony Eden was born at Windlestone Hall in County Durham in 1897 and was later educated at Eton and Oxford. After serving in the First World War he was elected as member of parliament for Warwick and Leamington in 1923. During his distinguished parliamentary career he became both Foreign Secretary and Deputy Prime Minister, which culminated in him being knighted in 1954. It was his short term in office as Prime Minister, less than two years, that contributed to his fall from power.

He made a tactical error in dealing with the Suez crisis following nationalisation of the Suez Canal by Abdel Nasser, the Egyptian leader. He achieved support from France and Israel for military action against Egypt's annexation of the canal, with an expectation that America would also support once action had been taken. Unfortunately American support failed to materialise and Eden had no option but to withdraw troops.

Above: *Sir Anthony Eden's Tomb in St Mary's churchyard, Alvediston.*

Left: *Low relief sculpture of Sir Anthony on a wall tablet in St Mary's church. Below the sculpture is engraved "Unshaken, unseduced, unterrified. His loyalty he kept, his love, his zeal"* (from Milton's *Paradise Lost).*

The blue Preseli Stone was transported from Cardigan to Amesbury by the Round Table.

Amesbury

Preseli Stone (SU 155 415)

The Preseli Stone is situated at the entrance to the town car park off the A345 in Amesbury. A carved inscription reads: "Itheaen Preseli, Teifi Valley. Amesbury Round Table 1981"

A metal plaque on the front of the stone explains the Welsh inscription and the reason for the stone's placement: "The Welsh inscription means Granite from the Preseli Mountain. This blue stone, a symbol of the Preseli stones which were laboriously transported from the mountain near Cardigan to Stonehenge about 3000 years ago was presented by Cardigan and Teifi Valley Round Table to Amesbury Round Table on 8th August 1981, marking the end of their sponsored haul."

The stone haul was organised by the Cardigan and Teifi Round Table, who undertook the same feat, but by mechanical means, to raise money for an appeal to renovate Stoke Mandeville Hospital in Buckinghamshire.

Five members of the Round Table dressed in animal skins with substantial beard growth, replicating the dress and appearance of prehistoric man, were given the task of moving the stone. They transported a nine foot block of blue dolomite granite with the aid of a tractor 180 miles from Cardigan to Amesbury. For obvious reasons the stone could not be added to those at Stonehenge, so it was left in the main car park at

Amesbury to be erected in its present location soon after.

The engraved inscription on the stone was carried out by Mervyn James, a mason from St Dogmaels near Cardigan.

Millennium Cross (SU 155 415)

For the millennium Amesbury erected a Celtic Cross, which is situated but yards from the Preseli Stone. A plaque on the cross states that it is a replica of the original cross and is the gift of T. G. Riggs and family. The supplier of the cross is engraved below the plaque and reads : "Gerald W. Burden".

The Celtic Millenium Cross has a typical cross and roundel head, but there is no Celtic engraving on the shaft.

The Amesbury Archer (SU 167 408)

The statue was designed by the Fire and Iron Gallery of Leatherhead. The head of the archer, cast in aluminium, was separately made by Masters and Munn and subsequently added to the Fire and Iron Gallery-manufactured torso.

The Amesbury Archer statue stands on a brick plinth near a small shopping precinct in the Archer's Gate housing development in Amesbury.

The discovery of the Archer's grave was made during routine excavation in May 2000 in advance of any building work on the Archer's Gate site, subsequently named after the importance of the grave finds. The skeletal remains have been radio carbon dated to between 2400BC and 2200 BC. The male skeleton was found curled up on its side, typical of finds dating from the time and was between thirty-five and forty years old when he died. In his later life he had suffered a traumatic injury to his knee, which would have given him a severe limp, putting much pressure on his right leg. Not withstanding the inevitable pain from his knee, his jaw showed evidence of a tooth abscess. He also had an unusual congenital deformity of his instep.

When fully excavated the grave proved to be the most important and well furnished interment from the early Bronze Age ever discovered. On the lower body were scattered 15 arrowheads, probably originally from a quiver of bow and arrows, the wood and leather having failed to survive. On his wrist was a stone wrist guard, used to protect himself from the recoil of the bow after firing an arrow. A similar guard was found by his knees. The most significant find among the grave goods were two gold earing-like objects, used either for ear adornment or for hair braids – there is some conjecture regarding this. Other goods consisted of copper knifes, a cache of flint tools, beakers and a kit of flint knapping and metalwork tools.

Gold and copper were new and important materials for the time, originating from within Europe. The inclusion of gold in the grave gave rise to the Archer being dubbed "The King of Stonehenge", the edifice standing but a few miles from where the Archer was buried.

A smaller companion grave to the Archer's was excavated, which contained a twenty-thirty-five year old man accompanied by a similar pair of gold objects. Peculiarly the instep of the man was also deformed with the same abnormality as the Archer, leading to the assumption that he was related.

The skeleton and grave simulation is on display at the Salisbury and South Wilts Museum in Cathedral Close.

The Ancestor (SU 173 421)

The home of the Ancestor at the time of writing is a prominent position on the green frontage of the Holiday Inn, Solstice Park, Amesbury. In order to finance its manufacture it has been put up for hire to promote events and causes in Wessex. In 2011 it was offered for sale on the E Bay auction website at a starting bid of £50,000 with a £1000 delivery charge. Since it appeared at an Olympic event and was sent back to Solstice Park in 2013, one assumes no one took up the offer.

The 24ft (7.3m) sculpture made from thousands of hand cut and welded steel pieces was made by Andy Rawlins and Michelle Topps. It was launched at the Stonehenge summer solstice of 2010 and in July 2012, holding a flaming torch, the Ancestor greeted the Olympic Torch relay at Hudson's Field in Salisbury.

A plaque at the Holiday Inn site reads:

"Ancient man on his knees, head thrown back arms open wide. Reaching up to the sky, spreading out like a mighty oak, straining towards the sun on the longest day. Rooted into the moon protected by three magical hares. The sun and moon with life in between. THE CIRCLE OF LIFE.

The Ancestor means many different things to many different people. This is what it means to us. *'We have forgotten to be grateful'*."

Andy and Michelle, A&R Metalcrafts.

The Ancestor outside the Holiday Inn, Amesbury.

A temporary move to Hudson's Field, Salisbury, to welcome the Olympic torch in 2012.

The Dragonfly is opposite the Holiday Inn, Solstice Park, Amesbury.

The Dragonfly   (SU 173 421)

The Dragonfly is the first of a number of permanent works of art at various locations within Solstice Park in Amesbury. It was created by Charlotte Moreton and apprentices from QinetiQ's engineering training centre at MOD Boscombe Down for the Salisbury International Arts Festival in 2007. A plaque names the 12 apprentices involved.

The inspiration for the art work was taken from the wild life of the River Avon, which flows through Amesbury. The body of the insect was made from an old Gazelle helicopter tail after making a model of the design involving months of commitment and hard work. The photograph is taken from the rear of the art work and clearly shows the upside down rotor housing at the rear of the helicopter.

The Dragonfly was officially unveiled on 11 June 2007 by Robert Key, MP for Salisbury, with an operational Gazelle helicopter overseeing the proceedings.

The Mallow (SU 176 422)

This is the second of the QinetiQ's apprentices' works of art at the Solstice Park site in Amesbury. The Mallow can be clearly seen in the park when passing on the A303 adjacent. I was unable to approach this artwork as it is positioned to the rear of an operational business company. However, it is on rising ground giving a clear photographic view, particularly with a zoom lens.

The Mallow is another Charlotte Moreton creation with the help of the apprentices from the third year in 2007/8. It is 8 metres tall and made from steel mesh.

It was unveiled in 2008 and is based upon the Salisbury Festival's theme for that year of vegetation and celebration, interpreting it as flowering and joy.

The Avon (SU 176 420)

The Avon sculpture consists of 105 vertical steel poles with heights ranging from 90cm to 2m tall. The artwork meanders like the River Avon for 30 metres. The dedication plaque also states that it represents the outline shape of the region's outstanding landmarks of Stonehenge, Old Sarum, MOD Boscombe Down and Salisbury Cathedral. I confess not to see the connection with the landmarks, with the exception, perhaps, of the spire of Salisbury Cathedral. In a photographic sense the most impressive parts of the sculpture are the shadows created by a late afternoon sun.

This was created by Charlotte Moreton with the third year QinetiQ apprentices at Boscombe Down for the 2009 Salisbury International Arts Festival with a theme of water. It was unveiled by Robert Key MP on 10 September 2009.

Another sculpture in Solstice Park represents the River Avon.

The steel mesh Mallow flowers besides the A303.

A different perspective on a Wiltshire White Horse from the QinetiQ apprentices at Solstice Park, Amesbury.

The White Horse (SU 171 418)

Salisbury International Arts Festival commissioned Charlotte Moreton for this, the fourth, sculpture with the third year apprentices at QinetiQ from MOD Boscombe Down. The 2010 Arts Festival theme was the region's white horses, which in this instance included the Uffington Horse, upon which this life-size sculpture is based. The stylized lines of the Iron Age horse are represented by floating plates on the Amesbury sculpture.

Charlotte Moreton and the QinetiQ apprentices designed, developed, built and tested the sculpture. An important training exercise to hone their skills for their future profession in the aeronautical industry.

The sculpture was officially unveiled on 21 September by Phil Harding of the *Time Team* television programme.

The Red Kite (SU 170 419)

The 2011 Salisbury International Arts Festival's theme was air and light. This is the fifth sculpture in the series of six which Charlotte Moreton and the QinetiQ apprentices designed and built. The sculpture gives the impression of the Red Kite gliding through the air with its iconic forked tail giving the bird of prey its distinctive appearance.

The QinetiQ Red Kite is poised in low-level flight over Solstice Park in Amesbury. This is the fifth of the sculptures commissioned from the apprentices at QinetiQ, Boscombe Down.

The sculpture is made of welded powder coated steel tubing and perforated steel plates and was unveiled on 4 October 2011 by the Mayors of Amesbury and Salisbury.

The Red Kite is an indigenous bird to the United Kingdom, but the population sank to just a few pairs in the west of Wales, south of Aberystwyth, by the 1930s. Although there was a slow recovery as the twentieth century progressed, the birds were high on the endangered list. In 1989 six Swedish birds were released in the north of Scotland together with four Swedish and one Welsh bird in Buckinghamshire. Further releases followed. From these small introductions the population growth has never looked back. I can only speak from personal observations of the bird in the south, but the range is slowly spreading west into Wiltshire.

To see a Red Kite in flight is magnificent, they glide through the air, often at low level, with their forked tail twisting to enable them to change direction. In the Thames Valley they are now common, probably being seen more often than the ubiquitous buzzard, even to the extent of dropping down into back gardens to feed on scraps thrown out for them.

Blade Henge (SU 173 421)

Blade Henge is the last of the series of sculptures in Solstice Park created by Charlotte Moreton and QinetiQ apprentices for the Salisbury International Arts Festival. It was inspired by Stonehenge and aircraft propeller blades. It is situated on the forecourt of the Holiday Inn within sight of both the Ancestor and the Dragonfly.

The sculpture is made from welded and powder coated steel tubing and plates and was unveiled by John Glen MP and Phil Harding on 11 March 2013.

Mosaic Mural (SU 166 408)

To celebrate Queen Elizabeth II's Diamond Jubilee a mosaic mural was placed within a curved wall at Archer's Gate in Amesbury. The mosaic also celebrates the history and wild life in and around Amesbury and was commissioned by Bloor Homes and Amesbury Town Council.

The mosaic was designed and constructed by Joanna Dewfall. The border was made by local adults and children under Joanna's guidance. Among the items depicted are the Ancestor, Stonehenge, early-to-modern aircraft, local archaeology, hares, the River Avon and the Great Bustard, which has been reintroduced onto Salisbury Plain. More of Joanna's work may be found in the Gazetteer under Salisbury.

Blade Henge is situated outside the Holiday Inn, Amesbury. The Ancestor with outstretched arms can be seen between the blades.

Spotlight on Boot Scrapers

Boot scrapers are present in most streets in Wiltshire and outside the doors of almost every church in the county. However, how many of the passers by and those entering a church to worship or admire its architecture and history even realise they are there.

There are myriad of designs, some are very ornate and definitely Victorian and others are simple and practical. Most elegant town houses have a cast iron boot scraper by the front door embedded in the step or pavement. A terrace of town houses may well have a scraper embedded in the wall next to each door.

All are redundant, but are often restored by the owners as relics of the past. Some of those recessed into a wall may be home to a flower pot and a geranium or a summer bedding plant.

Older Victorian school buildings usually had one or more boot scrapers by their entrance. Victorian children would invariably have been playing in muddy lanes or field footpaths on their way to school. It was advisable that two or more children could scrape their boots at the same time to avoid a bottleneck at the school door.

Where did the idea of boot scrapers begin? The practice of boot-scraping and the pride of owning the best examples began in Brussells, Belgium in the eighteenth century. They were known as "decrottoirs" or put very simply, excrement removers! They quickly caught on, as the streets were probably littered with horse dung from the principal mode of transport – horse drawn carts and carriages.

In the twentieth century with the introduction of motor vehicles and metalled roads and footpaths, the need for boot scrapers rapidly diminished in favour of the humble "Welcome" door mat.

Above left & centre: *Examples of embedded boot scrapers next to front doors in Malmesbury and Salisbury. The boot is scraped on the centre bar and the earth is removed with a shovel from a lower recess.* Above right: *Firmly fixed into stone is this ornate, probably Victorian scraper in Cricklade High Street.*

Below left: *A simple, but attractive design in Corsham High Street. The polished knobs suggested they were held while boots were pulled off one's feet.* Below centre & right: *Scrapers outside Cricklade, St Sampson's church and Aldbourne St Michael's respectively.*

  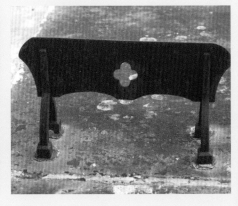

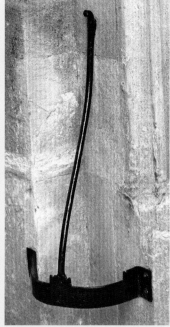

Above, left to right: *A boot scraper with hand rail at St John the Baptist, Charlton; the vertical support on the scraper at St Michael and All Angels can also be used as a steady; another hand steady scraper at St Cyriac's in Lacock.*

Below, left to right: *Hold the finial knob as a support while scraping your boot at Great Chalfield Manor; a freestanding scraper dated 1819 at St Michael and All Angels church in Mere – the two holes in the base are presumably for drainage.*

Above left to right: *Two persons' boots at once at St Peter's in Codford – the right hand scraper has more wear than the left; the priory church of St Mary, Saint Katharine and All Saints in Edington – remarkably this scraper shows signs of being used!*

Barberry Castle Country Park

Burderop Down – Jefferies and Williams Stone (SU 158 761)

This commemoration sarsen stone stands near the Ridgeway in the Barbury Castle Country Park. It commemorates two naturalists, Richard Jefferies (1848 - 1887) and Alfred Williams (1877 - 1930) and was placed there in 1939.

The plaque for Richard Jefferies reads: "It is eternity now. It am in the midst of it. It is about me in the sunshine." The passage is from *The Story of my Heart.* Jefferies was a prolific writer and wrote many books, which include *Toilers of the Field*, *Field and Farm* and *The Gamekeeper at Home.*

He moved to London in 1877, but he continued to write, reflecting on his childhood. He became ill in 1881 while living in Goring on Sea, but still continued to pen his books. He died on 14 August 1887 at the young age of thirty-nine.

There is a Jefferies Museum at his birthplace, Coate Farmhouse, south of Chiseldon, where original manuscripts and first editions of his work are held.

Alfred Williams is probably less well known than Jefferies, but was another, later, writer about the countryside. He lived in South Marston, near Swindon. His plaque reads: "Still to find and still to follow, joy in every hill and hollow. Company in solitude."

Jeffries and Williams Stone

Bemerton

George Herbert   (SU 121 307)

George Herbert (1593 - 1633) was a Welsh-born English poet, orator and an Anglican priest. He died at Bemerton in 1633 of TB (known then as consumption) and is buried in the chancel of St Andrew's church.

Briefly in 1624 and again in 1625 he served in parliament. When he was thirty-six he took holy orders in the Church of England and became rector at Fugglestone St Peter with Bemerton. Although his main church was at Fugglestone he lived in the rectory directly opposite St Andrew's in Bemerton. He was known for writing religious poetry – some of it being used in popular hymns.

In 2014 Salisbury held a George Herbert Festival with many events including readings. A circular engraved stone plaque, now fitted into the wall by the entrance door in the church porch, was blessed by former Archbishop Dr Rowan Williams.

Above: *St Andrew's church.*

Left: *"Love bade me welcome" plaque blessed by Dr Rowan Williams in 2014 in the porch of St Andrew's church, Bemerton.*

Right: *One of George Herbert's poems engraved on a plaque situated on the wall of the rectory opposite the church.*

Berwick St. John

Millennium Plaque
and Coronation Bus Shelter (ST 947 223)

In the village centre at Berwick St John are two commemorations, which stand adjacent to one another.

On the left is a rectangular pillar with an engraved record of the inhabitants of the village at the 2000 millennium. The village census registers that 227 souls lived in the village on that date. The plaque also records that the village is 472 ft. above sea level.

The second commemoration is a stone-built bus shelter for the infrequent Salisbury to Shaftsbury bus service. It was built for the Coronation of Elizabeth II in 1953 and is dated such. It has provided dry shelter for persons waiting for the bus, who can read the village notices placed inside, also away from the weather.

Box

Pinnacle Tomb (ST 823 685)

In the churchyard of St Thomas à Becket is a strange pyramidal type tomb called a pinnacle tomb. It was built for a husband, who under no circumstances, wanted his estranged wife to be able to dance on his gravestone in happiness about his passing. I know of no other in Wiltshire – unless the reader knows differently. I hope the estranged wife got the point, so to speak!

Another memorial at the church worthy of mention is to John Hanning Speke, the explorer who discovered a source of the Nile, after tracing the river to Lake Victoria in 1858, which he named after the Queen. Later it was discovered that another lake, named Albert was another source. Of course one could argue that the natives of the region already knew the source of the Nile and Speke was the first European to discover it!

Revd W. Awdry Plaque   (ST 827 688)

Reverend Wilbert Awdry OBE (1911 - 1997) was an Anglican cleric, a railway enthusiast and a children's author. He created the *Thomas the Tank Engine* series of books.

His association with Wiltshire began in 1917 when his family moved to Box, eventually settling at *Lorne Villa* (which they called *Journey's End*). The house was 200 yards from Box tunnel and the sight and sound of steam engines were to give Wilbert inspiration for story telling in later life, to his own son Christopher.

He told Christopher many stories about the exploits of the steam engines Edward and Thomas and eventually in 1945 his first book was published *The Three Railway Engines* followed by *Thomas the Tank Engine.* 26 books were published in all, until 1972 when he stopped writing. Christopher followed in his father's footsteps and added to the collection.

WILBERT VERE AWDRY
1911-1997
Clergyman and Author
lived here
1920-1928

The Poynder Fountain (ST 825 685)

A Grade II listed Gothic/Victorian drinking fountain dating from 1878 made of ashlar with pink granite columns and grey granite base with a bowl to the front and a trough to the rear.

A plaque describes the circumstances of its erection: "This fountain was erected in 1878 by William Henry Poynder Esq., Hartham Park, Wiltshire, and the site and supply of water to the said fountain was given by the Rev. E. Northey and Col. G. Northey for the use of the inhabitants of Box."

Surrounding the fountain is a low stone wall surmounted by railings. A gate has a plaque with the dates 1894 and 1994 together with Parish of Box in low relief. This obviously marks a centenary, but it is not made clear what event in 1894 occurred.

Bradford on Avon

Coronation Clock (ST 825 608)

The clock and associated iron work were made for the Coronation of Queen Elizabeth II in 1953.

I believe it was originally placed on a building called Westbury House. It was moved in the 1970s to the Lamb Building adjacent to Town Bridge occupied by a company called Avon, but when they vacated the building in 1992 it fell into disrepair and the iron work became rusty,

Fortunately at the time of the Queen's Jubilee in 2002 the Town Council decided to restore the clock and assembly. It was rededicated on 3 June 2002 by the Mayor. It was placed on St. Margaret's Hall. The hall was built in the eighteenth century as a dye house for the woollen trade. It was refurbished as a public hall in 1959 and the Town Council offices have been there since 2003.

Gold Pillar Box (ST 827 610)
and McKeever Bridge (ST 825 609)

It was Olympic year in 2012 and it was decided to paint one pillar box gold in the home town of all the winners of gold medals. The terms of reference for home town was that the winner must have been born there. In Bradford on Avon at the corner of The Shambles a double pillar box was painted gold in commemoration of Ed McKeever's win in the Sprint Kayak.

I will also mention at this juncture, the unofficial painted box in Larkhill for Captain Heather Stanning who was based in Larkhill, but wasn't born there. She won the coxless rowing pairs with Helen Glover. Overnight the postbox was painted gold by persons unknown. Compared to the box in Bradford on Avon it is very clear they only used 9ct gold paint! The Larkhill box has now turned back to red, but the Bradford box was still gold in March 2015.

Ed McKeever's achievement has also been celebrated by naming an existing footbridge across the Avon after him. There is a plaque on each side of the bridge.

The plaque placed on the footbridge across the Avon for Ed McKeever.

The footbridge across the Avon dedicated to Ed McKeever.

The gold pillar box in Bradford on Avon.

Unofficial gold box in Larkhill for Capt. Heather Stanning.

Edward Orpin Grave (ST 824 609)

The grave of Edward Orpin is just inside the graveyard wall of Holy Trinity church opposite Orpin's House, which has a Preservation Trust plaque attached. The bronze plate attached to the flat surface of Edward Orpin's tomb reads:

"Here lies Edward Orpin who died June 1781. He was the subject of the picture *The Parish Clerk* by Thomas Gainsborough PRA." Edward was the clerk of the market and his portrait is in the Tate Gallery.

Millie (ST 826 611)

Bradford on Avon has been associated with wool and cloth for three millennia. It was fitting in January 2000, at the dawn of a new millennium, to unveil a statue commemorating the town's association with the industry. The commemoration is a statue in the Festival Garden of a life size mill girl, which has been affectionately called "Millie".

The base of the statue simulates a Roman amphora to show the town's historical connection with the Roman era. On top of this is a drum with two angels, similar to those in the Saxon church and a fish, although termed a gudgeon, looks more like a perch. An inscription reads in Latin: "Sub Pisce Super Flumine", which translates to "Under the Fish (and) Over the Water". The fish and water reference is taken from the town motto, which is represented by the gudgeon weather vane on top of the lock up on the town bridge. Millie is releasing a dove to symbolise freedom and hope in the new millennium.

Millie's high waist band suggests eighteenth-century fashion and her hair is tied in a bun to prevent it being entangled in the mill machinery. The sculpture was the work of former town resident Dr John Willats.

The bronze statue of a mill girl stands in the town's Festival Garden. The inscription and artwork around the drum ring reads Sub Pisce Super Flumine or Under the Fish and Over the Water.

Bratton

Iron Works (ST 915 524)

There is a plaque and iron casting commemorating the site of Bratton Iron Works, R.&J. Reeves & Son, in the middle of the village in front of a green. The plaque records the existence of the works on the site from 1808 - 1972.

The company made agricultural implements and machinery of high quality. The plant had a foundry, smiths shop, fitting shop, tinsmiths and carpentry shop. In fact everything necessary to fabricate agricultural machinery from scratch.

An important folding and portable elevator was developed by Henry Reeves in 1896 for raising straw and hay for stacking. The iron casting above the plaque is one of a pair used on the elevator.

After the Second World War the company failed to compete with larger enterprises and eventually went into receivership in 1970, after which the works were completely demolished.

Bremhill

Maud Heath's Monument and Causeway (ST 974 739 - Monument)

Maud Heath lived in Langley Burrell, a village a mile or so from the centre of Chippenham, where she traded her eggs in the market a number of times each week. Apparently she did this for most of her life and became relatively wealthy in the process. On her way to market she probably met others going to town to buy and sell, who had walked from Bremhill and other villages east of Langley Burrell. In the winter this must have been a difficult journey across the Avon flood plain. Maud Heath had probably needed to travel this way herself

Top: *Maud Heath's column monument at Wick Hill, Bremhill.* Above: *A closer view of Maud Heath herself shows she is seated with her egg basket by her side.*

There is access to the surrounding railings at the base of the monument, which is prominently positioned on Wick Hill overlooking the route of Maud's path into Chippenham.

FROM THIS WICK-HILL
BEGINS THE PRAISE
OF MAUD HEATH'S GIFT
TO THESE HIGHWAYS

THE TRANSLATION INTO ENGLISH
VERSE OF THE EARLIER LATIN
INSCRIPTION ON THIS STONE WAS
MADE BY THE REV.W.L.BOWLES
VICAR OF BREMHILL IN 1827.

HITHER EXTENDETH
MAUD HEATH'S GIFT
FOR WHERE I STAND IS
CHIPPENHAM CLIFT.
ERECTED IN 1698. BUT
GIVEN IN 1474.

Top Left: *The plaque at the start of the Causeway at Wick Hill.*
(ST 974 739)
Top right: *Part of the 64-arch brick Causeway at Kellaways.*
(ST 947 758)
Lower Left: *The Kellaways monument and sundial. It has the*
words "Injure me not" engraved on the column and an erection
date of 1698, as well as the legacy. (ST 947 758)
Above: *The end of Maud Heath's Causeway in Chippenham Clift.*
I imagine Clift is an historical name for a part of Chippenham,
possibly Higher Chippenham. Some properties have Clift included
in their name. (ST 920 739)

on many an occasion. Some would have travelled on horseback, but this would have made the path even worse in bad weather for those on foot.

When she died in 1474, without issue, she left a legacy so that all could travel from the villages mentioned without walking through mud and rutted ground for miles to reach the market in Chippenham. The following words appear on the Kellaways sundial monument at the roadside: "In the year of grace 1474, for the good of travellers did in charity bestow in land and houses the sum of eight pounds a year forever to be laid out on the highway and causeway leading from Wick Hill to Chippenham Clift." This is known as Maud Heath's Causeway. The charity still maintains

the route at her bequest. The way was stone cobbled for the 4½ miles, which is probably under the present tarmac.

In 1811 the route was improved for those on foot by way of a 64-arch brick causeway at Kellaways, which would have been the worst part of the route prone to flood near the river. At the start of the Causeway is a plaque translated from the Latin by Revd W. L. Bowles, the vicar of Bremhill. In an adjacent field, surveying the landscape is Maud Heath sitting with her basket of eggs on top of a tall column. She is wearing simple clothing relative to the reign of Edward IV. At the base of the column engraved in the stone are the words of William Bowles (in his English):

"Thou who dos't pause on this aerial hight,
Where Maud Heath's Pathway winds in shade or light,
Christian Wayfarer in a world of strife,
Be Still and ponder on the Path of Life"

The column was erected in 1838 at the joint expense of Henry Marquis of Lansdowne, Lord of the Manor, and William L. Bowles, vicar of the parish of Bremhill.

Bowerchalke

Sir William Golding CBE (SU 019 229)

William Golding (1911 - 1993) was an English novelist, playwright and poet. He won the Nobel Prize for literature in 1983.

He was educated at Brasenose College, Oxford and achieved a degree in 1934. When the Second World War came in 1939 he served in the Royal Navy. After the war he became a schoolmaster at Bishop Wordsworth School in Salisbury, where he taught English.

His notable works include *Lord of the Flies* in 1954, which was made into a film in 1963, followed by a play in 1995, *Rites of Passage* for which he won the Booker Prize in 1980, *Free Fall* in 1959, *The Spire* in 1964 and *The Pyramid* in 1967.

He is remembered with three blue plaques, one at Bishop Wordsworth School in Salisbury on a gateway, another on a house in Marlborough, where he lived for a time and a third on a house in Mead End, Bowerchalke. He is buried in the churchyard at Bowerchalke.

Britford

Saxon Arch, Britford St. Peter's Church

The parish church of St Peter in Britford is Grade I listed and contains a Saxon nave with a round-headed arch from the Saxon period, c. ninth century, which leads to a small porticus. The south side of the arch is plain, but the north side (pictured) is decorated with stone slabs. The tiles between the Saxon work are believed to be Roman in origin.

The carving of interlaced vine scrolls seems to be inspired by earlier work on the Bewcastle Celtic cross from Cumbria and the Ruthwell cross from Dumfries and Galloway in southern Scotland (in Saxon Britain it was part of the Kingdom of Northumbria).

The church also has the Radnor family mausoleum attached dating from 1764 with alterations in 1873, providing ashlar walls and a pitched roof.

Top: *The grave of William Golding in Holy Trinity churchyard, Bowerchalke.*
Above left: *The heritage blue plaque remembering William Golding's days as schoolmaster in Salisbury Cathedral Close (SU 145 296).*
Above right: *The heritage blue plaque in Marlborough where he used to live (SU 190 693).*

The north side of the Saxon arch in St Peter's church in Britford.

Broadchalke

Sir Cecil Beaton's Grave (SU 040 253)

Cecil Beaton was a fashion, portrait and home front war photographer. He supplemented his photography with stage and costume design for both film and theatre. He was knighted in 1972 and won Academy Awards for his costume design in the media of film.

He was born in Hampstead on 14 January 1904 and starting learning photography with a Kodak 3A owned by his nanny. Education was at Harrow and St John's

College, Cambridge, but Cecil left without a degree in 1925. An attempt was made at office work, but he had no interest in paperwork and struck out on his own with his beloved photography.

Personal recognition was sought in America and he built up a reputation in New York, which resulted in a steady flow of work. He returned to the UK and photographed the blitz in London during the Second World War, then leased Ashcombe House in Wiltshire. In 1947 he purchased Reddish House near Broadchalke.

He worked for the top fashion magazines, which included *Vogue* and *Vanity Fair* and photographed many top celebrities throughout his career. He won acclaim for costume design for the films *Gigi* (1958) and *My Fair Lady* (1964), winning Academy Awards. He died in Reddish House on 18th January 1980 and is buried in All Saints' churchyard in Broadchalke.

The pedestal of the cross for Thomas Moore has the following inscription:

"Dear harp of my country, in darkness I found thee
The cold chain of silence had hung o'er thee long
When proudly, mine own island harp, I unbound thee
And gave all thy chords to light, freedom and song."

Bromham

Thomas Moore (ST 964 652)
and Millennium Cross (ST 964 651)

Thomas Moore (1779 - 1852) was an Irish-born poet, singer, songwriter and an entertainer. He is probably better known in Ireland and more particularly in Dublin, his birthplace. He is known for the lyrics for *The Minstrel Boy* and *Last Rose of Summer*.

He settled in Sloperton Cottage in Bromham, where he became a novelist, biographer and poet. He was a close friend of Byron, whose words are on the base of the cross: " The poet of all circles and the idol of his own".

The Millennium Cross in Bromham is situated close to a children's play area and was sculpted by Headington sculptor Chris Fixsen. In 2006 it was vandalised and knocked over leaving only a stump in situ. The 15ft. high monument has since been repaired. Close by is an engraved stone commemorating the planting of an oak tree by HRH The Prince of Wales and HRH the Duchess of Cornwall on 7 July 2007.

The Millennium Cross at Bromham. It has MM engraved on the base of the shaft.

Calne

Chavey Well (ST 995 709)

Chavey Well is in the Castlefields Canal and River Park. A plaque records the purity of the water and that it was the only safe water in Calne during an epidemic, probably of typhoid, between 1880 and 1890. Note the high relief sculpture of a boar's head on the wall. When dogs go "walkies" along the adjacent path they cannot resist a dip in the cold water, hence the damp patches all over the paving!

The Chavey Well is situated alongside the old Wilts and Berks Canal branch to Calne.

Above: *The double ring of Scots Pines.*

Left: *The Diamond Jubilee plaque leading to Queen Elizabeth II Field.*

Queen Elizabeth II Field (ST 997 708)

In Castlefields Canal and River Park, possibly on or near the site of an ancient castle in Calne, is a double ring of Scots Pines.

The tall inner ring was planted to commemorate the Diamond Jubilee of Her Majesty Queen Victoria in 1897. The saplings growing in an outer ring were planted by the Marquis of Lansdowne, LVO, DL, Vice Lord-Lieutenant of Wiltshire to commemorate the Diamond Jubilee in 2012 of Her Majesty Queen Elizabeth II.

Barometer (ST 997 710)

On the front of the Georgian façade to the Lansdowne Strand Hotel in Calne is reputed to be the largest wheel barometer in England.

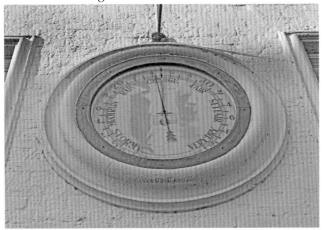

The hotel has its origins as the Catherine Wheel Inn with (presumably) several attached houses in its make up, possibly dating from the late sixteenth century. It was a coaching inn in the eighteenth/nineteenth century and the barometer may have been placed later in the nineteenth century to advise passengers with regard to the weather prospects on their way to Bath.

The building is Grade II listed, but bizarrely the barometer is not mentioned, but an undated clock in a moulded surround is!

Bronze Pigs (ST 997 712)

Calne has had a long association with the Harris factory producing pork and bacon products. To celebrate this connection a sculpture of two pigs was created by local sculptor Richard Cowdy for the Calne Civic Society, who gave the sculpture to the town.

The Harris business was founded in 1770 and grew steadily until it dominated the town with factory buildings. The business employed 2000 people, which was 20% of the town's population. At its peak it processed

The Calne Pigs in Phelps Parade, Calne town centre. The ears are clearly tactile having developed a shiny patina with human touch.

5000 pigs per week, turning them into all manner of meat products. By 1980 C&T Harris was a subsidiary of FMC Ltd., who, as a result of rising costs and regulation decided to close the factory in 1983. The town was devastated by the news of their largest employer closing down. The factories were knocked down and the town centre redeveloped. Calne is now beginning to prosper again and is certainly a more attractive place to visit without the domineering presence of high walls, but this is a matter of opinion.

The Head (ST 998 700)

The stainless steel head simply titled "The Head" is built from small welded stainless steel platelets on a lattice work frame. The brain area has no steel plates to cover it and it supposedly is meant to represent the challenges of the future.

This is a modernist sculpture by Rick Kirby, who first worked in carved stone, but now almost exclusively uses steel, often stainless. Most of his work is of the human form. Other sculptures include "Mask" at Marlow Theatre, Canterbury, "Arc of Angels" at Portishead and "Cross the Divide" at St Thomas' Hospital in London.

The Head glints in the sun and looks impressive lying on its side in front of the library in a paved area by the Lansdowne Strand.

The stainless steel Head by Rick Kirby is situated outside Calne Library.

Scaffold Motorbike (SU 006 729)

On the outskirts of Calne situated in a field adjacent to the A 3102 from Calne to Wootton Bassett is a very large motorbike sculpted with scaffolding tubes cut to varying lengths and joined together with scaffolding fittings.

It was built by Toby Welsby to publicise the 2013 Calne Motorbike Meet. It represents a Royal Enfield bike and is very clever in its conception. The bike itself is 15ft. high and 26ft. long and used many hundreds of yards of pipe in its making.

The Calne Bike Meet takes place in July each year when the town is taken over with motorbikes arriving from all directions.

Bronze Sheep and Lamb   (ST 998 712)
The life size bronze sculpture of a sheep and lamb is the work of Richard Cowdy. The sculpture sits in the fore-court of Sainsbury's and is set surrounded by Baggerbridge cobblestones in a geometric pattern representing the many crop circles that appear in the Wiltshire corn fields.

The whole area around Sainsbury's was once the Harris pork meat factory. Following the demolition of Harris's and the regeneration of the site, the Sainsbury forecourt design came about by a joint venture between Sainsbury's and the Calne Artists Group. A bronze sheep and lamb were chosen to reflect Calne's heritage as a centre for the broadcloth industry of the eighteenth Century.

Tile Annulus (ST 997 708)
In Calne Castlefields conservation area the Calne Artists have created an artwork of individual tiles set in an annulus around the base of a sapling tree. The artwork celebrates thirty years of the Calne Music and Arts Festival. The tiles are on a theme of music and natural history. While I was taking this photograph of the tiles, a local informed me that that due to vandalism the tree had been planted five times!

Bronze sheep and lamb by Richard Cowdy situated in the forecourt of Sainsbury's in Calne.

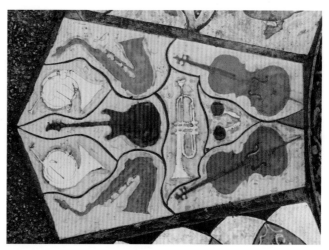

The annulus of tiles celebrating music and artists in Calne and (above) one of the elements of the annulus showing various musical instruments

Bas Reliefs (ST 998 711)

Built into a stone wall by a stream through the centre of Calne are a number of bas reliefs. They are on a theme of life, which of course could not survive without oxygen, the breath of life, which Joseph Priestley discovered in Calne.

The figure (top), is of course, not Priestley, but Darwin. Charles Darwin was a naturalist and geologist, most famous for his theory of evolution and his book written in 1859 *The Origin of Species*.

The bas reliefs are credited to Richard Cowdy and Vivien ap Rhys Price.

Joseph Priestley (ST 998 711)

A bronze plaque to Joseph Priestley (1733 - 1804) is the centrepiece of a pavement mosaic in a small seating area commemorating his discoveries. The mosaic is credited to David Reeves, Chris Fixsen and Vivien ap Rhys Price, members of the Calne Artists Group.

He was born in the West Riding of Yorkshire, near Leeds. He studied at the Dissenting Academy at Daventry and his subjects included philosophy and

Pavement plaque of Priestley in the centre of a mosaic commemorating his discoveries.

science. His family where dissenters (not conforming with the Church of England) and he became deeply interested in religion. After leaving the Academy he ministered between 1755 and 1761 and was ordained as a dissenting minister in 1762. He also taught languages and literature.

Science became very important to him and he was involved with experiments in electricity and the chemistry of gases, for which he is best known. He discovered ten new gases, which included nitrogen, oxygen and carbon monoxide. However, oxygen was independently co-discovered by Carl Willhelm Scheele.

In 1773 Priestley moved to Calne to take up a position as librarian and tutor for William Petty, Earl of Shelburne and his family. In 1780 he moved to Birmingham to become a preacher and joined the Lunar Society, which counted among its members, Josiah Wedgewood, James Watt and Mathew Boulton. His support for revolutionaries in France and dissenting in general eventually contributed to the Birmingham riots of 1791, during which Priestley's home was burnt to the ground, causing the family to move south. In 1794 he moved to America and his preaching led to the founding of the First Unitarian Church of Philadelphia. Although he continued scientific research he became out of touch with developments in Europe. He died in Pennsylvania in 1804.

Jan Ingen Housz   (ST 998 700)

At the library entrance in Calne is a commemorative pavement plaque to Jan Ingen Housz MD, FRS (1730-1799). He was Dutch and a doctor to the Austrian Royal Family, but he was in England in 1779. He spent the summer of that year conducting experiments, in a house near London, proving that plants absorb carbon

The Walter Goodall George plaque on the Town Hall.

Top: *The pavement plaque outside the library entrance.*

Above: *The heritage plaque for Dr Jan Ingen Housz in Calne (ST 998 710).*

dioxide and release oxygen in sunlight – thus purifying the air we breathe. We call this photosynthesis. He returned to England in later life after retirement and often stayed in Bowood House where he died.

Walter Goodall George (ST 997 710)

Walter George (1858 - 1943) was an athlete, born in Calne, specializing in the mile. As an amateur he achieved numerous world records over various distances. He was champion of England winning the mile in 1879 in a time of four m 29 sec. He went on to improve on this time the following year to achieve just over four m and 23 sec.

In 1881 professional William Cummings achieved a little more than four m 16 sec. The target was set and George turned professional in 1885 in order to challenge Cummings. This he did and won in a little over four m 20 sec. In 1886 they raced again and George set a new world record of four m 12.75 sec. This was to stand for nearly thirty years. The time was beaten, I believe, by an amateur in 1915.

Sydney Wooderson was the first Briton to better George's time in 1935 and went on to achieve four m 6.4sec in 1937. The plaque was unveiled by Sydney Wooderson on the centenary of George's achievement.

The four minute mile was broken by Roger Bannister in 1954. The mile record set in 1999, still current in 2015, is held by Hitcham El Guerrouj with a time of three m 43.13 sec. – an unimaginable time in 1886. The mile is the only non metric race for which records are universally accepted.

Cherhill

The Lansdowne Monument (SU 048 693)

Prominently on the top of Cherhill Down, to the right of the Cherhill White Horse, stands the Lansdowne Monument. Unfortunately it is in a poor state of repair and the large stepped plinth is boarded up to prevent access. The monument's exposed position lends itself to erosion from the elements. The corner stones of the pillar are visibly damaged and there is a danger of falling masonry. A notice on the monument explains the repairs necessary. The Bath stone quoins (corner stones) will be replaced with Doulting stone, which is more suited to outdoor exposure. Funding wasn't available at the time of my visit in 2014, so, when the structure will be returned to safe condition is unknown.

The Lansdowne Monument seen from a circular walk taking in the Cherhill White Horse and Oldbury Hill Fort. Note the protection against falling masonry surrounding the monument.

There is a commemorative plaque on the monument, which is presently inaccessible, but a copy of the wording is posted on the exterior boarding. It reads: "Designed by Sir Charles Barry and built in 1845 by the 3rd Marquis of Lansdowne in memory of his ancestor Sir William Petty (1627 - 1684) physician and surveyor. Repaired by the National Trust in 1990 with funds raised by public appeal and grants from Historic Buildings and Monuments Commission."

The home of the Lansdowne family is Bowood House, which is about 4 miles from Calne. The gates of Bowood House were also designed by Charles Barry, who, with Pugin, were co-architects of the Houses of Parliament.

Sir William Petty qualified as a doctor and was appointed Professor of Anatomy at Oxford. Acting as Physician-General to Cromwell's army in Ireland he was the first to conduct an accurate land survey of the country. He was a founding member of the Royal Society and founder of the Lansdowne family's prosperity.

The chalk downland here is ideally suited to wild flowers and butterflies, From the high point there are excellent views in all directions. The Cherhill White Horse is covered in the Spotlight on White Horses.

Millennium Sundial (SU 034 700)

A thatched and oak substantially-built bus stop erected for the Millennium, which has a sundial to the rear.

In the centre of the sundial is a vertical pointed sarsen and a rectangular tiled circumference has Roman numerals within. The pointing between the tiles theoretically gives finer time divisions. However, there is a major problem of encroaching shrubbery, making the casting of a shadow impossible. It had, unfortunately, an unkempt appearance when I photographed it.

One hopes the bus timetable isn't based on the casting of a shadow at a given time!

Chicklade

Cratt Hill – BAC 1-11 Crash (ST 905 360)

On 22 October 1963 a BAC 1-11 aircraft on a test flight crashed on Cratt Hill killing all on board. There is a memorial to the crash and the seven crew on board situated above Chicklade, one mile along a country track with public access, but there are parking difficulties and no access to the site by car.

The test flight of G-ASHG met with disaster twenty-three minutes after taking off from Wisley. The test pilot, Mike Lithgow was testing the aircraft's recovery from a stall, it was the fifth test of the day. The plaque on the memorial states the aircraft was flying at 17,000ft when it entered a "deep stall". It descended very quickly in a horizontal attitude and struck the ground with very little forward speed and pancacked. The plane caught fire and all the crew perished. Modifications were made to the "T" tail elevators and the leading edge of the wings, correcting the problems.

Those on board were: Lt Cdr M.J. Lithgow O.B.E. - Project Test Pilot; Capt. R. Rymer - Test Pilot; B.J. Prior - Assistant Chief Aerodynamicist; C.J. Webb - Assistant Chief Designer; R.A.F. Wright - Senior Flight Test Observer; G.R. Poulter - Flight Test Observer; D.J. Clarke - Flight Test Observer.

There is an apt quotation from Samuel Taylor Coleridge at the base of the plaque: "… and everywhere the blue sky belongs to them and their appointed rest and their native country."

Top: *The crash site at Cratt Hill of BAC 1-11 registration G-ASHG.*

Above: *BAC 1-11 Royal Aircraft Establishment registration XX 105. This aircraft was previously G-ASJD, which in 1964 had to make a forced landing on Salisbury Plain.*

Mike Lithgow was Chief Test Pilot for Vickers Supermarine. He held the World Speed Record in 1953 with a Supermarine Swift at 735.7 m.p.h. During the war he flew Swordfish torpedo bombers and piloted one of the aircraft attacking the *Bismark*.

Less than a year later on 20 August 1964, prior to delivery to British United Airways, another BAC 1-11 had to make a forced landing on West Lavington Down on Salisbury Plain. This was G-ASJD, which after a rebuild joined British United's fleet in August 1965, followed by some time in the service of British Caledonian after which it joined the RAE fleet as XX 105.

Despite these setbacks, the 1-11 was a successful aircraft and retired more due to noise abatement than obsolescence.

Chilmark

Millennium Cross (ST 969 326)
The Chilmark Millennium Cross has an oak shaft and a Chilmark stone base. It is placed on the possible site of a medieval preaching cross. There are inscriptions around the larger base plinth showing the names of all families living in the parish on 1 January 2000.

The dedication for the cross is on the smaller of the stone plinths and reads:

"A cross stood near here in medieval times and provided a site for prayer and meetings. The new cross, of English oak and local stone, was erected by the people of Chilmark with help from Salisbury District Council, to commemorate the Millennium and was unveiled by HRH the Prince of Wales on 27 June 2000."

The carpenter for the oak cross was David Beck and the stonemason was Mark Luscombe.

Chippenham

Bronze Calf (ST 921 733)
Richard Cowdy's bronze calf titled simply "Calf" is situated near the entrance to the old nineteenth-century Cheese Market in Chippenham. A plaque placed below the calf explains the significance of the animal to Chippenham, recognising the importance of the cattle markets to the history of the town.

Chippenham Civic Society commissioned the calf sculpture from Richard Cowdy and it was unveiled in 2013. The sculpture had only been in place less than a year when I photographed it. Already the tactile nature

The Calf by Richard Cowdy is situated in the entrance walkway to the nineteenth-century Cheese Market in Chippenham.

Fox Talbot and his subjects, a little girl and her dog. It is unusual to have separate elements of the same sculpture so far apart, but that's the nature of photography.

of the animal's ears encouraged passers by to run their fingers over them, in similar fashion to the Calne pigs.

Chippenham was home to one of the largest cattle markets in England. It was held in the Market Place until 1910, then it moved near to the Neeld Hall. It was finally relocated to Cocklebury Road, near the railway station, away from the town centre. The cattle market closed permanently in 2005.

Fox Talbot and Subjects (ST 915 749)

A statue of William Henry Fox Talbot and his photographic subjects stands on a green within the Greenways Business Park in north Chippenham. A plaque describing the sculpture comes straight to the point: "William Henry Fox Talbot (1800 - 1877). Father of modern photography and inventor of the negative in 1835. Sculptor Greta Berlin. Commissioned by Timberlaine Properties Plc. Unveiled by Anthony Burnett-Brown".

Of course modern photography now uses digital imaging to capture the subject, but when the sculpture was installed in c.1993, film was still king. It is ironic that I used a digital camera to capture this study of Fox Talbot using his primitive camera to produce a negative image.

Fox Talbot's photograph of the lattice window at Lacock Abbey was the earliest use of a negative to produce a positive image. The negative required lengthy exposure to fully develop the image on translucent paper. He improved the exposure time with the calotype process where a latent negative image on translucent paper was subject to further chemical development out of the camera. By contact printing using the negative with sensitized paper any number of positive images could be processed from one single negative.

Later glass was used as a carrier for the photographic emulsion, dramatically improving sharpness of the image. There is a Fox Talbot museum at Lacock Abbey.

Greta Berlin is well known for her figures, which she

has drawn and sculpted for over forty years. Her other public works include: "Sidmouth Fiddler" in Connaught Gardens, Sidmouth and "Skateboarder" at Wimborne Minster.

The Twister (ST 920 735)

The Twister stands near the north bank of the river Avon in front of the council offices in Monkton Park, Chippenham. It is sculpted from Bath stone and has local children's figure drawings over the spiral form.

A plaque reads: "The Twister. Bath Stone. 21 September 1995, By Lorraine Frost. Drawings by local children."

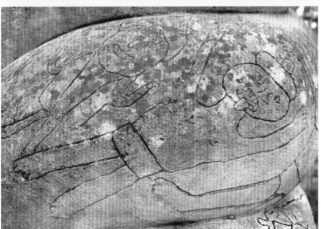

Buttercross (ST 922 732)

A modern replacement for the original Chippenham Buttercross erected in the present position by the Chippenham Civic Society in 1995 and paid for by donations from various Wiltshire councils, charities, trusts and private companies.

The first Chippenham Buttercross was built in c.1570 in the position where Barclays Bank now stands. It was in the centre of the Butchers Shambles and used for selling meat and diary produce. It was sold for the sum of £6 in 1889 to a Mr Lowndes, who used it as a garden gazebo in Castle Combe Manor House. The design of the new structure was by N.W.D.C. Architects.

Chippenham Butter cross.

Eddie Cochran (ST 911 726)

Pop idol between 1955 and 1960, Eddie Cochran, died after a road accident on the A4 at Chippenham while on his way to London Airport with Gene Vincent and song writer Sharon Sheeley. He was taken to a hospital in Bath, where he died on 17 April 1960.

A memorial stone and plaque is located on the verge of the footpath next to the road at Rowden Hill, Chippenham, where the taxi in which they were travelling crashed into a lamp post. Both Gene Vincent and Sharon Sheeley survived the crash, The driver of the taxi was later banned from driving for fifteen years and fined £50 for speeding, according to contempory news reports.

On the fateful evening of 16 April Eddie Cochran had performed at the Bristol Hippodrome during his British tour and was, presumably, starting his journey home to America with Gene and Sharon. Eddie Cochran is best known for his hit songs *C'mon Everybody* and *Summertime Blues*.

The roadside memorial for Eddie Cochran.

Millennium Clock (ST 917 740)
and Monkton Spring (ST 922 733)

Intended for the Millennium celebrations in Chippen-ham, a news report in 2008 stated that the Millennium Clock had been installed in John Coles Park eight years late. For reasons unclear the clock installation had not been proceeded with in time for 2000. It was a priority for the Mayor in 2008, Sandra Oakes, to see the clock installed and a plaque on the clock pedestal records this event.

The clock was donated to John Coles Park by Sheldon School to celebrate the Millennium.

The Monkton Spring casting has the following words: "This water was given to the town of Chippenham by G.M. Esmeade Esquire and the expense of conveying it to this spot was defrayed by Sir John Neeld Bart. James Wharry Mayor, October 1864."

An abundant spring of water rose from one of the islets in the river near Town Bridge. The water was granted to the town by the owner of Monkton and it was piped under the river to the bridge where it rose to the Monkton Spring casting bowl.

Left: *The John Coles Park Millennium Clock.*

Below: *The Monkton Spring is now outside the Yelde Hall as a feature.*

Chippenham High Relief Classical Figure Work
(ST 921 731)

Three nude figures in classical poses are placed above the upper storey windows of the Castle Lodge retirement home near the bus station in Chippenham. The home was built in 2005 as retirement apartments for the over sixties. The figures are in high relief and are already showing signs of surface deterioration.

Information on the figures is scanty. The central figure of the three has two theatrical masks, the purpose of which, on retirement apartments, is obscure.

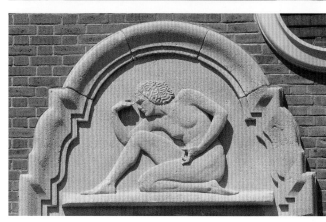

Chiseldon

Centenary Stone   (ST 188 798)

This sarsen is a bit of a mystery. It has a low relief dagger/spear head symbol within a circle and the dates 1075-1975 engraved below the circle. Originally there

was a rectangular fabricated stone base around the sarsen situated at the height of the "tide mark".

The village of Chiseldon is mentioned in the Domesday Book, perhaps 1075 is the first record of habitation in Chiseldon. It is situated on the site of the old M.S.W.J.R. station between Andover and Cheltenham.

Clatford Bottom

Devil's Den (SU 152 696)

Devil's Den is the remains of a Neolithic long barrow about 230 ft. long. The appearance today is of a dolmen, sometimes referred to as a cromlech, the result of recon-struction in 1921 of the remaining stones. A long barrow would have had an entrance, a stone-covered passage and one or more burial chambers. In some cases the internal structure was of wood leaving no solid remains. However, the presence of stone slabs indicates that wood was probably not used in Devil's Den. It is, there-fore, assumed most of the stones belonging to the barrow are no longer present, having been used over the centuries for other purposes. Furthermore the raised long barrow is no longer obvious, having suffered erosion as the result of agriculture.

The site is very close to the sarsen stone field of Fyfield Down. The dolmen is accessed through a gate into a small fenced field to which the public have access. Despite probably not representing its original form, it is an attractive feature in the landscape and worthy of the walk to visit it, particularly as the sarsen stone field can be included in the venture,

One may enquire why this structure has acquired the name of Devil's Den. In the past when the long barrow was more obvious and perhaps more complete, there must have been a great deal of mystique and myth surrounding the structure. Before it was attrib-uted as the home of the devil the barrow was known as Dillion Dene. Analysis of the name gives us Dillions, meaning a series of heaps of soil on the Wiltshire downs representing border markers and Dene meaning valley.

Thus the barrow becomes a heap of soil in the valley (Clatford Bottom). It is easy to see that with a Wiltshire dialect and a good slice of supernatural superstition that Dillion Dene becomes Devil's Den over time. I doubt many locals visited the place after dusk!

Devil's Den in Clatford Bottom

Colerne

Richard Walmesley Monument (ST 870 711)
The monument was erected in 1893 by subscription to record the grateful appreciation of the many benevolent acts of Richard Walmesley of Lucknam. On the top of the monument's column is a sundial and on the base is engraved P. Sheppard, Colerne, who one assumes was the mason.

The Walmesley family bought Lucknam Park in 1870. Richard was a Victorian squire who helped the poor and funded many local building projects. His son followed in his footsteps. Lucknam Park was sold in 1918.

Above: *The Walmesley Monument in Colerne village.*
Below: *The benevolent nature of Richard Walmesley is aptly stated.*

Collingbourne Ducis Golden Jubilee commemoration and Collingbourne Kingston Coronation commemoration.

Collingbourne Ducis and Kingston

Golden Jubilee Commemoration (SU 244 538)
The village of Collingbourne Ducis celebrated the Golden Jubilee of Queen Elizabeth II with a steel cross and crown.

Coronation Cross (SU 239 557)
The Coronation Cross at Collingbourne Kingston is not the original commemoration for the 1953 Coronation. A Coronation Stone was placed in this location in 1953, but it was demolished by a lorry. In 1992 the Parish Council erected a wooden cross surmounted by a crown in replacement.

There are two plaques on the cross, one explains the reason for a new commemoration and the other, a circular tablet, commemorates the Collingbournes twinning with Le Merlerault in France.

Coombe Bissett

Plague Stone (SU 279 263)
The Plague Stone in Coombe Bissett is a flat slab depressed in the centre. Such a stone was used in time of plague and pestilence as a place for relatives and friends to leave communications and parcels of food to avoid contact with the villagers, which could spread the disease present in the village community to the wider population.

In 1665 the village of Eyam in Derbyshire was devastated by plague. A bundle of cloth ordered from London by the village tailor had fleas present in the parcel. A large proportion of the village became infected with plague and the village chose self isolation to prevent spread of the disease. It took fourteen

The Coombe Bissett Plague Stone is situated in the centre of a short footway which crosses over the river Ebble.

months for the Eyam epidemic to end. A stone slab was used to leave and collect communications with the outside world, situated at the fringe of the village In this connection the Coombe Bissett stone may have been moved to its present central position in the village from the edge of habitation at some time in the past, now to become a feature and talking point of the village.

It was over 300 years earlier, in 1348, that the epidemic of "Black Death" (bubonic plague) reached Wiltshire. It was carried by fleas on black rats spread by merchant shipping from Europe. By 1350 over 30% of the population of Britain and Europe had died as a result of plague. The plague of 1665 probably did not reach the Salisbury area as King Charles II fled from London to stay at Malmsbury House in Salisbury Cathedral Close to escape the pestilence.

The disease is circulated mainly by fleas on small rodents. With no effective medicine at the time, plague was deadly. The disease is caused by the yersinia pestis bacteria. The first signs after infection occur within three to seven days when flu-like symptoms develop; fever, headache and vomiting. This is followed by swollen and painful lymph nodes in the area where the infection entered the skin. The lymph nodes may break into open sores, Without treatment death occurs with 30-80% of those infected, who die within ten days.

The infection also causes gangrene where the finger tips, toes, lips and nose effectively die. The infection can spread to the lungs where it becomes pneumonic plague. The disease is still prevalent in Africa where a cure is achieved by antibiotics, but we learn from the medical profession that disease is beginning to learn how to combat our ultimate cure and become resistant. One can only hope that a vaccine is developed that is 100% effective and eliminates the disease from the face of the earth for ever.

Corsham

Peacock (ST 872 703)

Peacocks are featured in the town logo and that of the Chamber of Commerce. The birds can sometimes be seen in the town streets and certainly can be heard when walking in the direction of Corsham Court, where they roam freely.

In the Martinsgate shopping precinct situated on a wall above a community noticeboard is a mosaic peacock. It was designed by a Heywood School pupil and the school children helped to create it. It was unveiled in 2014.

Lion (ST 872 703)

Near the Peacock Mosaic, in the shopping precinct is a Lion, which at the time of my photograph was adorned with a map of Brazil and a number of flags, which had almost worn away, probably by children's stroking hands. I imagine the Lion is made of fibreglass and resin and stands on a metal plinth. It seems to take on various guises depending upon significant world community events, like the Olympics in 2012, when it was painted gold. This was the result of a competition to give the Corsham Lion a new look, which was organised by the owner of a local shop.

On my last visit the Lion was not present and I am not sure whether it was being redecorated or retired.

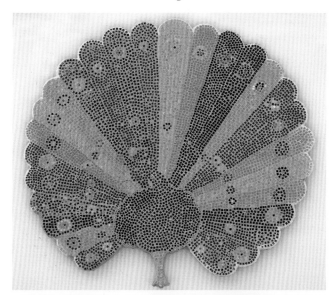

Sarah Jarvis and New Teeth (ST 874 706)

The grave of Sarah Jarvis is in the churchyard of St Bartholomew. A plaque is placed in front of the grave repeating the inscription on the flat slab table tomb, which is difficult to read. I quote: "In memory of Sarah Jarvis who departed this life the 11th day of December 1753 in the hundred and seventh year of her age. Some time before her death she had fresh teeth."

To live to 107 in 1753 must have been exceptional and even more so to have and afford new teeth at any age in the eighteenth century. In the early years of dentistry false teeth were made from ivory or even authentic teeth from another person (probably dead!). In the Museum of London are a set of teeth made from hippopotamus ivory (I think this must be their tusk teeth). Apparently it was common to remove your teeth while eating. The probable reason for this is that their ill fit would cause them to come out stuck to a leg of chicken or an apple perhaps – not a happy thought! Towards the end of the eighteenth century it was more commonplace to have false teeth made of porcelain.

Water Fountain (ST 873 706)

A drinking fountain built during Jubilee year, 1897, in honour of Charles Mayo (1834 - 1895), a local dignitary. He was a prominent Liberal, Vice Chairman of the Parish Council and a public speaker on subjects ranging from education to India.

In 1887 he was a member of the committee responsible for the town's Jubilee celebrations. He was chairman of Corsham Water Works and was involved in bringing piped water to Corsham in 1889.

He is remembered on the south porch of the church with three sculptures. See later entry in the Gazetteer.

Water fountain.

Queen Victoria Diamond Jubilee (ST 873 706)

Queen Victoria's Diamond Jubilee was commemorated in Corsham by placing a stone medallion and commemorative text over the doorway of the Town Hall. The relief text has suffered some erosion since it was placed there in 1897. It reads: "The above clock and medallion were erected in commemoration of the sixtieth year of the reign of H.M. Queen Victoria."

The Town Hall was built as a Market Hall with open arches in 1783. It was subsequently enclosed to house a lock up. The upper storey was added in 1882 and it was used as a military hospital in the First World War.

St Bartholomew's Porch Figures (ST 874 705)

On the south porch of St Bartholomew's church in Corsham are three figures set in niches. They are St Bartholomew, the patron saint of the church, St Peter holding a traditional key and St Paul with a sword and book. They are dedicated to the memory of Charles and Mary Mayo and the Revd Robert Mayo recorded on a discoloured engraved stone tablet, which states the figures were placed in their positions in 1919 on St Bartholomew's Day.

St. Bartholomew died in the first century AD. He was flayed and crucified in Armenia. St Bartholomew's Day in the Anglican Communion is on 24 August.

Queen Victoria Diamond Jubilee commemorative text and medallion.

Above: *The discoloured memorial tablet on the church porch.*

Left, from left to right: *St Bartholomew, St Peter and St Paul.*

Sir Michael Tippett (ST 872 704)

Sir Michael Tippett (1905 - 1998) was an English composer whose reputation flourished during the late twentieth century. He studied at the Royal College of Music between 1923 and 1928.

His major works include *A Child of Our Time, The Ice Break* and *King Priam*. He wrote four symphonies, various orchestral, operatic and choral works.

He moved to Corsham in 1960 when he had started to work on his opera *King Priam*. He spent much time on this work often at the expense of other compositions he had in his pending file. He moved from Corsham to a secluded house in the Marlborough Downs in 1970.

Tippett was a pacifist and applied for registration as a conscientious objector during the war, but after various hearings and statements from some of his well known musical friends, he was given a three month prison sentence. He was released early and not bothered again.

for by public subscription is situated where Cricklade's Town Cross once stood. The internet town guide states that replicas of the cross are now in both St Sampson's churchyard and St Mary's. Both crosses look old enough to be originals and the county history states it was moved from the High Street to St Sampson's churchyard.

The cast iron clock pillar has a maker's plate of Searle and Company, 78 Lombard Street, London, EC.

Queen Victoria's Diamond Jubilee clock in Cricklade.

Milkman's Memorial (SU 102 939)

Gordon Bridges must have been a very well respected milkman to warrant a memorial and a seat by the river Thames in Cricklade. It is in a small seating area by Thames Bridge and is on the rear wall by the right hand seat. If someone is sitting in the seat it cannot be seen.

There is also a commemorative plaque for the Thames Bridge restoration. On the wall on the left hand side of the photograph is a panel for North Wall, which I assume refers to the town's Saxon ramparts.

Above: *Corsham pedestrianised High Street. One doesn't need to ask upon which house the Tippett plaque is placed.*

Left: *Sir Michael Tippett plaque on the wall of a house in the High Street, where he once lived for ten years.*

Cricklade

Jubilee Clock (SU 099 934)

Outside the Vale Hotel in Cricklade High Street stands an attractive pillar clock. It was erected in 1898 to celebrate Queen Victoria's Diamond Jubilee the preceding year, having been monarch since 1837. The clock, paid

Above: *The seating area in which the plaque is placed.*

Left: *The Gordon Bridges plaque, which is very small and can easily be missed.*

Millennium Wood Stone (SU 107 937)

The stone is standing next to the infant Thames by the Thames Path and mentions that it is necessary to cross the bridge (out of the picture on the right) to reach the Millennium Wood. The wood was planted by the people of Cricklade to celebrate the Millennium.

Further planting has taken place to celebrate the Jubilee, together with a wild flower meadow.

The Millennium Wood standing stone.

Diamond Jubilee Mosaic (SU 099 935)

To celebrate the Queen's Diamond Jubilee in Cricklade a floor mosaic was laid in 2012 as the centrepiece of a seating area in a community garden known as Saxon's Rest, so called because of the town's Saxon origin – Alfred the Great built it as a fortified town in the ninth century. The garden itself was opened in 2009.

The mosaic shows the town's coat of arms surmounted by a spray of snake's head fritillaries, which grow in profusion in North Meadow Nature Reserve in spring – well worth a visit. In the border is a design of Saxon-style artwork.

The Town Council appointed Debbie Stirling, a local artist from Cirencester to undertake the mosaic with a design by the Cricklade Art Group.

The Jubilee Mosaic in Saxon's Rest.

Crudwell

Stained Glass Commemorations (ST 956 929)

There is good collection of glass from medieval to modern in Crudwell All Saints church. The panels featured here are commemorating the Golden Jubilee of Queen Victoria in 1887 and the second millennium in 2000.

The Victorian window has six main character features. From left to right in the upper lights then the lower lights: the glorious company of Apostles; Christ, the King of Glory; the goodly fellowship of the Prophets; the noble army of Martyrs; all Angels; and the world's churches showing acknowledgment.

Above and below: *The stained glass window and plaque inside Crudwell church commemorates the Golden Jubilee of Queen Victoria.*

Above right: *The Millennium Window in Crudwell church was created and installed by Colin Stokes with funds provided by the people of Crudwell.*

Spotlight on Domesday – 1086

In 1986 commemorative plaques were placed in settlements mentioned in the Domesday Book of 1086. The Book records 337 place names and landowners within the boundary of Wiltshire. The plaques are not always easy to find. The example shown below right is at Upton Lovell (ST 944 409). Another at Hilperton, near Trowbridge, is seen on a wall near and opposite the blind house (lock up). I have passed this one many times without noticing it (ST 872 593). Another I had found, before embarking on this book, is at Fisherton de la Mere (SU 001 385). Quite how many places have Domesday plaques in Wiltshire, I am unsure, but it would be interesting to search for more.

The Domesday records were planned and set in motion in 1085/6 by William the Conqueror, who sent assessors to each Shire with terms of reference to record the location of habitation, to determine property ownership, their livestock and asset valuation. It was written in medieval Latin and was used to calculate how much tax was owed. Some parts of northern England and Wales were not included, probably because they had not been conquered yet! London and Winchester were exempt from tax and were not assessed.

The Domesday Book is the oldest public record in England. To refer to the record as one book is not strictly correct as there exist two volumes of the work. They are referred to as the *Little* and *Great Domesday Book* and are held in the National Archives at Kew. *Little Domesday* comprises Essex, Norfolk, and Suffolk and the *Great Domesday* the balance. Why was "Domesday" chosen to be used as the name of the survey? "Domesday" is an old English version of "Doomsday" and was chosen because the survey ordered by William I was considered the final authority.

Above: *The village water pump and Domesday plaque in Hilperton, near Trowbridge.*

Right: *A typical Domesday plaque placed in places of habitation in 1986 that existed at the time the Domesday Book was written in 1086.*

ISSUED TO CELEBRATE NINE HUNDRED YEARS OF NORMAN HERITAGE

This Community is recorded in the DOMESDAY BOOK 1086

DOMESDAY 1086-1986

Authorised by the NATIONAL DOMESDAY COMMITTEE

HUNDRED: Melksham

POPULATION: 234 Households

VALUE TO LORD IN 1086: £ 113·6

HOUSEHOLDS: 92 Villagers, 66 Smallholders
            35 Slaves, 31 Freedmen

OTHER RESOURCES: 8 Mills, 1 Church

LORD IN 1066: Earl Harold

LORDS IN 1086: Rumold the priest, King William

(Entry 1 Domesday Book)

Left: *On an exterior wall of The Milk Churn in Melksham is a record of the entry in the Domesday Book regarding the Hundred of Melksham.*

It is interesting that eight mills were required for a relatively small population. Also that there were 35 slaves. The Romans introduced slavery to Britain and the practice was continued by the Saxons. At the time of the Domesday Book about 10% of the population were slaves, the result of capture in conflict, takeover by a new ruling elite or submission due to famine. By the end of the twelfth century the practice had largely stopped.

Above: *The small village of Fisherton de la Mere is mentioned in the Domesday Book. The photograph shows St Nicholas church, which is no longer used for services but is preserved under the Churches Conservation Trust. The church is often the oldest building in the community; although St Nicholas was rebuilt in 1833, there is evidence of Norman work in the chancel arch according to Pevsner.*

Below: *Another village mentioned in the survey is Maddington. This photograph was taken in 1909. The cottage on the right has a plaque commemorating the great flood of 1841. See under Shrewton in the Gazetteer, where Maddington flood cottages are mentioned.*

Devizes

Cloth Factory Tympanum (SU 005 616)

The Trust for Devizes has placed a plaque conveniently on a wall near the tympanum to enable the observer to identify all of the subject matter worked by the sculptor, Eric Stanford A.R.B.S. The sculpture was presented to the town through the Trust for Devizes enabled by a bequest from one of the late members, Neil Williams.

John Anstie erected the cloth factory in 1785. It was one of the earliest factories to manufacture woollen cloth in the West of England. The tympanum shows an arc of sheep with shepherd, his dog and wool shears and the various items of machinery and the tools used to manufacture the cloth. In the centre is a conjectural portrait of John Anstie – there may have been no official painted portrait of him. Immediately below the portrait are a group of teasels, the dried seed head of a plant used to comb (tease) the cloth.

The plaque was unveiled by Denis Anstie, a descendant, in October 1998.

The tympanum over the entrance to the old cloth factory in Devizes.

The Pyramid (SU 007 615)

The bronze Devizes Pyramid is the work of sculptor Richard Cowdy of Calne, well known in the area for his Calne pigs and sheep sculptures. The three faces of the pyramid show three aspects of the town's history, trade and transport. The photograph shows sides depicting the castle and Wiltshire sheep. Wool being important to the town for its cloth making activity. The remaining side of the pyramid shows the Caen Hill flight of locks on the Kennet and Avon Canal, an important waterway route to Bristol and London before the coming of the railway.

The sculpture was presented to the town by Patrick and Joan Norton of Long Street, Devizes and unveiled in 2008. The architectural consultant to Richard Cowdy was Anthony Bolland of Devizes.

A plaque records the following information on the town: Devizes is derived from the Latin term "ad divisas", meaning at the boundaries. Devizes stands at the three manor boundaries of Rowde, Potterne and Bishops Cannings.

The bronze Devizes Pyramid.

High Reliefs, 4/5 St John's Street (SU 004 614)

On the corner of St John's Street with Wine Street and currently occupied by a bank is an ornate building dating from 1912 with modern ground level alterations. The upper storey has florid stucco and a scalloped copper-domed lantern on the roof. The piers are embellished with high relief heads each set in a wreathed circular recess based on characters from the history of Devizes. From left to right starting in St. John's Street and working round into Wine Street the figures in sequence are:

Roger, Bishop of Sarum. He was Chancellor and Treasurer to Henry I. After the wooden Devizes Castle burnt down in 1113, he rebuilt the castle in stone c. 1138.

Matilda. She laid claim to Stephen's throne after the death of Henry I. This resulted in civil war in the 1140s. Stephen was defeated and Matilda ordered an attack on Stephen's former stronghold of Devizes Castle.

Hubert de Burgh. He was a great Justinian, interpreted as a believer in the body of civil law set out by the Byzantine (East Roman) Emperor Justinian I. After a disagreement with Henry III he was imprisoned in Devizes Castle in 1233.

Edward I (1239 - 1307). Known as Edward Longshanks, he made visits to Devizes Castle during his reign.

Ralph Hopton. A Royalist Civil War commander with a garrison in Devizes Castle. He played a part in the Battle of Roundway Down in 1643. This was a

The ornate upper storey of 4/5 St. John's Street, Devizes.

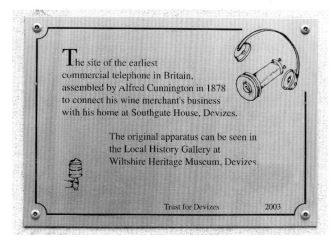

The site of the earliest commercial telephone plaque in Devizes.

commercial telephone was used in England.

The telephone consisting of separate headphones and mouthpiece was assembled by Alfred Cunnington to connect his vintner's business with his home. He had made the equipment from descriptions by Edison in *Scientific American*.

The original apparatus Cunnington made is in the Wiltshire Heritage Museum, which is a few hundred yards further along the road.

The Crammer Pond (SU 010 615)

All Wiltshire folk are called Moonrakers for the reason explained on the plaque overlooking the Crammer Pond. It is a legend, but nevertheless one that makes Wiltshire folk proud to be living in the county. The plaque tells the story succinctly and I quote:

"The origin of the Crammer is not known and neither its name, which was probably derived from Cranmere, meaning crane pond. However, it has often been associated with the famous Wiltshire Moonraker Legend, bestowing the nickname on the county's inhabitants.

"The story goes that some Wiltshire smugglers who had concealed kegs of brandy in the pond were observed by excise men in the moonlight in the act of trying to retrieve the kegs. The moon was reflected on the water and the smugglers said they were trying to

The Crammer Pond.

significant Royalist victory against higher odds.

Sir Thomas Lawrence (1769 - 1830). He was a leading portrait painter and president of the Royal Academy. His father was an innkeeper and moved to take over the Black Bear Inn in 1773. Thomas Lawrence spent his childhood there.

Site of Earliest Commercial Telephone (SU 005 614)

A brushed metal plaque can be found on the wall of a building in St John's Street, Devizes, placed there by the Trust for Devizes. It records the site where the earliest rake out 'thik gurt yaller cheese.' Convulsed with laughter, the excise men rode on, while the smugglers chortled, 'We were too vly for they. There baint no vlies on we.'"

The pond is owned by Devizes Town Council and is a popular spot in the summer with children. The plaque was the gift of Mr John Drake, Mayor of Devizes in 1972/73, who was made an honorary freeman of the town in March 1996.

Market Cross (SU 004 615)

The Market Cross was erected in 1814, replacing an earlier example. A plaque dedicates it to Henry Viscount Sidmouth as a memorial of his attachment to the Borough of Devizes of which he had been Recorder for thirty years and of which he was six times unanimously chosen as a representative to Parliament.

The Corn Exchange can be seen to the rear of this photograph. Before this was built, the sacks of corn to be traded were piled around the base of the Market Cross.

Also recorded on a plaque on the Market Cross is the tale of Ruth Pierce, who was accused of cheating some buyers in the Market Place in 1753. After the incident a board with painted letters telling the story was placed in the market place to deter others from cheating. This was later replaced by a sign affixed to The Bear. When the new Market Cross was erected, a plaque detailing the story was placed upon it, only the tale was embellished to provide a moral when one may not have existed. The plaque tells this story:

"On Thursday the 25th January 1753, Ruth Pierce of Potterne in this County, agreed with three other women to buy a sack of wheat in the market, each paying her due proportion towards the same. One of the women, in collecting the several quotas of money, discovered a deficiency, and demanded of Ruth Pierce the sum which was wanting to make good the amount. Ruth Pierce protested that she had paid her share and said, 'She wished she might drop down dead if she had not.' She rashly repeated this awful wish; when to the consternation and terror of the surrounding multitude, she instantly fell down and expired, having the money concealed in her hand."

The coroner was unable to find any obvious cause of death and declared that she had been struck down by the vengeance of God. There is no evidence or record to suggest that Ruth Pierce had money clutched in her hand when she died. It is most likely that the trauma of accusations and surrounding crowd triggered Ruth Pierce to have a heart attack, causing her to collapse, in which case any money clutched in her hand would likely have been released, clattering around her as she fell. Thus it is possible that Ruth Pierce could have been falsely accused and one of the other women may have been responsible – we will never know.

Water Fountain (SU 012 616)

A water fountain is situated on the corner of London Road with Brickley Lane. A plaque is inscribed : "The gift of J.J. Fox to the Borough. November 1st 1868." J.J. Fox were cloth manufacturers and retail drapers.

On the base of the water fountain are inscribed the words: "This corner was presented to the Borough of Devizes in memory of Frederick Robbins. November 18th 1898." A Frederick Robins is recorded in the 1861 census as a master brewer.

Millennium Cross (SU 004 612)

The Millennium Cross is situated in St John's churchyard and was commissioned by the Trust for Devizes, Wiltshire Archaeological and Natural History Society, St John's Church and the Town Council. It was sculpted by local sculptor Eric Stanford. It shows local scenes and activities from the town's history.

It was damaged by vandalism with a hammer in 2006, chipping pieces away from the shaft and crunching some of the scenes. It has since been repaired at some expense. See also damage to Bromham Cross.

Drowning Memorial (SU 004 612)

In the centre of the churchyard at St John's, close to the Millennium Cross is a 15ft high obelisk, which is a memorial to five young persons who drowned in a boating accident on 30 June 1751 – they are interred below the obelisk.

The inscriptions are worn and difficult to interpret, but the five met their end in Drew Pond on the outskirts

The Market Cross.

The Fox Water Fountain.

Millennium Cross.

Drowning Memorial.

of Devizes at Roundway. There were three beer coolers lashed together at Drews Pond, which were used by anglers, presumably to get to a favoured fishing spot. Six persons boarded the "raft" and floated out into deeper water. The raft was unstable and the coolers upturned throwing them into the pond. Only one of the party survived, the rest drowned.

Estcourt Statue and Fountain (SU 004 615)

The statue of Thomas Sotheron Estcourt (1801 - 1876) is poised on a pillar, which is part of a substantial water fountain, in Devizes Market Place. It was unveiled in September 1879 as a memorial to Thomas Estcourt who was MP for Devizes between 1835 and 1844

Estcourt was a Conservative and became MP for Marlborough between 1829 and 1832. Subsequent to him representing Devizes he was elected MP for North Wiltshire and served between 1844 and 1865. In 1859 he was appointed Home Secretary. He founded the Wiltshire Friendly Society.

The whole fountain structure including the statue is Grade II listed. In view of the complex nature of the water fountain as a whole it is preferable to quote the description from the listing: "Consists of a large stone octagonal basin with sides of inverted segmental curves and angle piers and crowned with bronze eagles with secondary smaller drinking troughs on each face with lion mask spouts. From the centre of the large basin a massive central shaft of grouped, curved formation supports an upper basin, from which a tall group of engaged columns rises in centre forming base of statue."

The Thomas Estcourt statue stands on a group of engaged columns in the centre of the water fountain.

Statue of Ceres (SU 004 615)

The statue of Ceres stands proudly on the top of the Corn Exchange and is showing signs of erosion being in such a prominent exposed position overlooking the Market Place since 1857.

Ceres is the Roman Goddess of agriculture, grain and crops – hence Goddess of the Harvest, a fitting figure to crown the Corn Exchange. The sculpture was paid for by Christopher Darby-Griffith MP.

Ditteridge

St Christopher (ST 818 695)

In 1854 during work on the interior walls of St Christopher's church, fragments of a very good fresco were discovered. The fresco was that of St Christopher fording a stream with the Christ child on his back carrying an orb. On the lower right was a mermaid looking into a mirror.

There is a reproduction of the fresco inside the church. The original fragments were not conserved at the time and disappeared after a while due to exposure to air.

Above left: *The statue of Ceres overlooks the Market Place in Devizes. Pigeons also use it as a high vantage point to survey and swoop down to tidy up crumbs left by snacking tourists.*

Above right: *A reproduction of St Christopher and a vain mermaid in Ditteridge church.*

Downton village cross.

Downton

Downton – Village Cross (SU 176 215)

The Village Cross is situated in the Borough and for that reason it is locally called the Borough Cross and sometimes the Memorial Cross. The stepped base is probably medieval judging by the depressions on the steps indicating centuries of footfall and usage of the steps as seats. No doubt its first use would have been as a preaching cross and a meeting point.

It has been reconstructed a number of times over its existence. It is thought that the cross was knocked down in Cromwell's time and by enemy action in the Second World War. It was last reconstructed to celebrate the Coronation of Queen Elizabeth II in 1953. The main pillar is clearly modern, but the small cross at the top was found at the time of reconstruction and may be original.

Downton holds a Cuckoo Fair in the Borough every year and the stepped base of the cross is used by children as a vantage point to view the proceedings.

Downton – Millennium Green Sundial (SU 175 205)

The Downton Millennium Green Sundial is situated in a public area beside the River Avon created to commemorate the Millennium. This type of sundial uses a vertical gnomon, in this case a person and is known as an analemmatic sundial.

In the centre is a rectangular block with the months of the year inset in brass. Within the boundary circle of the sundial are two ellipses of numbers, one ellipse for October to March and another for April to September. The position of the months and the numbers, representing the time of day, are calculated using mathematical formulae depending upon the declination of the sun at given times of the year and the location of the dial. A person stands on the month position in the centre rectangle and the shadow cast shows the time.

Downton – Millennium Beacon (SU 182 215)

The Downton Beacon is in the centre of a small green at the top end of the village virtually opposite Barford Lane. It was first ignited for the National Millennium Beacon Event on 31 December 1999 at 12.00 midnight, the turn of the century. I have no doubt it will be lit for significant events in the future. Unfortunately it is not situated on a high spot and is unlikely to be seen from a long distance.

Millennium Sundial and detail.

East Knoyle

Sir Christopher Wren (ST 882 306)

Christopher Wren was born in 1632 in East Knoyle, near Mere, where his father, also Christopher, was rector. There is a commemorative tablet framed in stone standing on a stone plinth on a small green in the centre of the village. The plaque reads: "In a house

Top: *The Christopher Wren monument in the village centre.*
Above: *A portrait of Wren on the village shop.*

Architecture was a natural progression from his inventive and technical background. In 1664 Wren accepted a commission to design the Sheldonian Theatre in Oxford. A year later plague hit the City of London with a vengeance, followed by the Great Fire of London in 1666. Much of the City was completely destroyed giving Wren a golden opportunity to put his recently established architectural skills to the fore. Wren designed over 50 new churches and of course the magnificent St Paul's Cathedral. He was knighted in 1673 before his final design for St Paul's was accepted. There followed many important commissions of which the Royal Observatory at Greenwich and Chelsea Hospital were two of the most significant.

He died in 1723 and is buried in his masterpiece, St Paul's Cathedral. On his memorial is written in Latin:

"LECTOR, SI MONUMENTUM REQUIRIS,
CIRCUMSPICE"

Which translates:

"READER, IF YOU SEEK A MONUMENT -
LOOK AROUND YOU"

East Tytherton

Maud Heath Sundial (ST 966 749)

A substantially-built vandal proof (hopefully) stone sundial erected for the quincentenary (500th anniversary) of Maud Heath's Causeway 1474 - 1974.

Another sundial associated with Maud Heath is on St Peter's church, Langley Burrell.

near this spot was born on 20th October 1632, Sir Christopher Wren, architect, mathematician, and patriot, the son of the rector of this parish."

The reference to patriot on the plaque, no doubt referred to the fact that the family were staunch Royalists, which caused them some difficulties during the English Civil War.

The Wren family moved to Windsor in 1635 for Christopher Wren senior to take up the position of Dean of Windsor. Christopher junior was sent to Westminster School in London for his education and later to Wadham College, University of Oxford. He showed a great interest in the sciences, mathematics, astronomy and his own inventions.

In 1657 Wren was appointed Professor of Astronomy at Oxford. A year later, along with fellow mathematicians and scientists, he helped found the Royal Society.

Edington

The Edington Millennium Commemoration Stone.

Millennium Stone
(ST 927 531)

To celebrate the Millennium the village of Edington placed a sarsen stone in the green centre of a small road island. A plaque on the stone celebrates the past of the village and looks forward to the future.

Ford

Millennium Seat (SU 163 329)

The seat sculpted out of stone, probably from Chilmark, is situated by the River Bourne close to Ford Watermill. Engraved on the stone seat back is the wording "Ford Millennium" and a waterwheel. Ford watermill dates from c 1783. I have never seen anyone sitting upon it, despite passing it regularly – probably too cold and dank.

Ford commemorated the Millennium with a stone seat.

The Sarsen Stones resemble a flock of grey wethers. They are scattered over a large area on Fyfield Down. When I visited the area on foot from Fyfield with my wife, Liz, we walked through a green lane absolutely swarming with butterflies, delighting in the heady scent of privet blossom. More small tortoiseshells than I had ever seen.

Fyfield Down

Sarsen Stones   (SU 140 703 typical)

On Fyfield Down between Marlborough and Avebury is a significant quantity of boulders lying erratically on the down, these are called Sarsens. Although there are a large number of sarsens scattered on the downs west of Marlborough, the best assemblage is north of Fyfield village in a shallow valley, probably the result of past climatic conditions. Here they lie in sufficient quantity that one can practically leap from one to another. However this practice is not recommended, as the sarsen concentration is part of a nature reserve and the stones are protected.

The stones are marked on the ordnance survey map as "Grey Wethers", which is an alternative term for sarsen stones. Close together they resemble a flock of grey sheep, hence the term "wether". The dictionary definition of a wether is a male sheep, more usually rams that have been castrated.

In prehistoric times the quantity of sarsens lying on the downs would have been significant. Their exposed position and individuality in size and shape caused them to be selected by Neolithic and Bronze Age man for stone circles and burial chambers. Throughout millennia sarsen stone has been used as building material and in recent history for commemoration features, particularly in Wiltshire villages, where irregular but attractive shaped stones with a dedication plaque have been used to commemorate significant events.

Sarsens are composed of hard silicified (cemented) sandstone laid down in Tertiary sediments between c 65 million and c. 2 million years ago. The sediments covered an under layer of chalk, which over time have eroded away, but harder cemented lumps that have resisted erosion remain scattered on the downland landscape. The harder lumps in the sandstone sedimentary layer are the result of patchy dissolved silica evaporating in the warm climate of the time, cementing the grains together.

The derivation of the word "Sarsen" may well be from "Saracen", a name associated with myth and magic – the stone of the pagans.

Spotlight on Guide Posts, Old Road Signs and Topographs

Guide posts are also referred to as finger posts because the arms of the posts direct as a finger pointing the way. Sometimes the arms of the post actually have fingers at their extremity. The dictionary definition is a post with one or more arms or fingers pointing in the direction of travel with mileage to the destination marked on the finger.

The posts can be made of wood, cast iron, steel or recycled plastic. With the exception of the plastic posts, all are painted, usually with black and white banding on the post with white arms and black lettering for roads and other colours for footpaths, cycle tracks and specialised purposes. Wiltshire has a specification for all its new wooden posts, which details the quality and type of timber, the size and profile of the timber and the painting procedure.

In 1697 legislation was enacted enabling magistrates to place direction posts at cross tracks (the highways of the day). In 1766 a Highways Act and a Turnpike Roads Act in 1773 made finger posts compulsory on turnpikes.

The original wooden guide posts have failed to withstand the test of time and the elements, but later cast iron still stands as a testament to the quality of manufacture. Examples are the Grade II listed guide post dating from the mid nineteenth century standing in Tisbury, opposite Hazeldon Old Manor and another at Rowberry near Ludwell. Both were manufactured by John Farris of Shaftesbury.

In town and city centres there are often guide posts to twin towns and places with the same name, but on different continents. Most are recent additions to signage and all will be "as the crow flies." There are unexpected places only short distances down the road, such as Scotland, Ireland and even New Zealand. Near Bremhill a signpost is completely blank, leading to nowhere! A trifle misleading, perhaps, as it featured on an inn sign called the *Dumb Post Inn*.

During the Second World War many guide posts, milestones and other identifiers of location were removed. Such an action was necessary in the event of a German invasion, so an invading army would not easily be able to locate themselves. Having said that, the enemy were just as able to read maps as we were! I suppose some signs were turned to add confusion. In the final event, all the tactics to confuse an enemy that did not reach our shores with marching boots proved unnecessary.

Included in this spotlight on route indicators are the old signs pre the Warboys report of July 1963. The Government-sponsored Warboys Committee under Sir

Above left: *The current standard design of a Wiltshire guide post in wood (SU 156 478).*
Above centre: *Metal guide post used as an interim design between wooden types – common around Wiltshire (SU 303 551).*
Above right: *Grade II listed guide post at Hazeldon, near Tisbury (ST 934 280).*

Above left: *A cast iron guide post at Rowberry near Ludwell. The Shaftesbury arm looks like a modern replacement as it is in pristine condition and the lettering is not in an identical font to its neighbouring arm. (ST 921 230). Above centre: An example of the wooden Wiltshire guide post design, but with fingers at the end of each arm, the only one I have found like this in the county, although there could be others. (ST 978 867). Above right: Another cast iron design in Ham with Shalbourne unusually marked as one mile, 1st on the left (SU 331 631).*

Above left: *A recycled plastic guide post on Overton Hill marking the start of the Ridgeway Path and signposting Ivinghoe Beacon at 87 miles away (SU 121 681). Above centre left: A shorter than average cast iron guide post in Semley. It is festooned with place names and mileages. An interesting question to fox the children would be: how many miles are recorded to the places on the arms? Adding them up there are 33 and ½, but of course there are the miles to add on the reverse of the arms! (ST 892 269). Above centre right: A lamp standard serving also as a guide post in Pewsey (SU 169 602). Above right: Another lamp standard and guide post in Tisbury (ST 945 292).*

Above left: *Between North Bradley and Southwick, Scotland is only quarter of a mile away and Ireland but half a mile. This post is a replacement of one that also marked the mileage. It is a great shame the mileages were not included (ST 849 549). Above centre: A National Cycle Network guide post at Chiseldon south of Swindon, it is situated on the old Midland and South Western Junction Railway line between Swindon and Marlborough. Route 45 goes between Salisbury and Chester and Route 4 from London to Fishguard (SU 193 794). Above right: In Salisbury Market Square is this long distance direction and mileage finder. It has the twin towns in Europe of Saintes (France) and Xanten (Germany) marked, together with sister cities in North Carolina and Maryland in the USA (SU 145 300).*

Top left : *The inn sign for the* Dumb Post Inn *suffering the effects of damp (ST 976 728).* Top right: *Still retaining its road identity plate bolted on to the guide arm is this post in Swindon (ST 148 838).*
Above left: *Very much the worse for wear is this pre -Warboys road sign on County Road, Swindon. The road number identity plates are missing. I am informed that they would have been A 361, A345, A420 and A419. I am not sure if this has been forgotten or there is a future intention to preserve it (SU 157 853).* Above right: *Another pre-Warboys sign in Ramsbury (SU 275 716).* Right: *In Hindon the road left leads to the A303. The black and white hatched stripe above the road number indicates it is the route towards the numbered road (ST 910 329).*

Walter Warboys, chair of ICI, reviewed all the signage on British roads and the subsequent report suggested radical changes, which were implemented.

For obvious reasons I am omitting signage post the report, as we are all familiar with that. Becoming scarce are signs before the report and for some odd reason Swindon features in most of those that are still extant, either directing to Swindon or still existing within the Swindon area.

I now turn to viewpoint markers or topographs. These are usually situated on high ground with a panoramic view radiating in front of the observer. Such viewpoints are marked on ordnance survey maps as a small semi circular or circular blue radiant symbol. Not

all such locations will benefit from a topograph.

So, what is a topograph? It is a word derived from topography, the arrangement of the natural and physical features of an area. The topograph itself is a stone monument upon which is situated an engraved metal plate showing the direction and distance of notable features in the landscape, which may be geological features or larger places of interest.

A topograph will show the points of the compass, but it will obviously depend upon the location as to whether the observer has a 360 degree view or not. In some locations a telescope may be provided. Not all locations will be accessible by road and public footway meaning walking may be necessary to reach them.

Above: *Liddington Castle topograph and triangulation stone with view over Swindon and Highworth (SU 210 798). A permissive path leads from the Ridgeway.*

Below: *Topograph and view from Mere Castle Mound (ST 809 326). A stiff climb to the top.*

Above: *The topograph on Pepperbox Hill with view north (SU 213 249). Car park then on foot.*

Below: *Win Green Hill topograph near the white triangulation stone (ST 925 207).*

Above: *The view from Harnham Hill topograph overlooking Salisbury (SU133 287). Accessible only via footpath above Harnham.*

The topograph next to Westbury White Horse (ST 898 514). Car park opposite.

Great Bedwyn

Jubilee Lamp Standard (SU 278 645)

Situated on a small traffic island at the junction of High Street with Church Street, this ornate lamp standard celebrates Queen Victoria's Jubilee in 1887.

It is Grade II listed, which describes the lamp standard as follows: "Cast iron lamp standard with drum showing moulded crests. A complex shaft of various features terminating in a Corinthian capital. Ladder arm and hexagonal lantern with a crown finial. Electrified. Placed on the site of Great Bedwyn Town Hall, which was demolished in 1860."

Farm Lane, which is close by, was renamed Jubilee Street for a time around the 1887 Jubilee, but has now resumed its old name. How long it carried the name is not known, but it could have been until the turn of the century, as there was another celebration in 1897.

Stone masons (SU 278 644)

Exhibited outside Great Bedwyn post office are a number of monumental mason's pieces attached to the walls. They commemorate the Lloyds Mason's yard adjacent to the post office that was once filled with monuments and masonry artwork. It was in fact a stone museum of mason's work.

Lloyds was established in 1790. The family at the time were involved in the construction of the Kennet and Avon Canal and were also involved with building the school in 1835.

In 2009 the company was reorganised and sold items from the yard including statues, a Roman sarcophagus and some dinosaur footprints. The museum was closed when I last visited Great Bedwyn.

Here lies John Higgs
A famous man for killing Pigs
For killing Pigs was his Delight
Both morning Afternoon and Night
Both heats and Colds he did Endure
Which no Physician could ere Cure
His knife is laid His work is Done
I hope to Heaven his Soul has Gone

Top:
The post office with masonry work exhibited.

Above:
I know not whether John Higgs existed or not, but a good epitaph.

Left:
An ornamental gravestone - the work of a master mason.

Thomas Willis (SU 280 646)

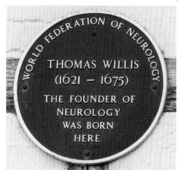

There is a plaque on Castle Cottage in Farm Lane recording the birthplace of Thomas Willis, known as the Father of Neurology.

Thomas Willis (1621 - 1675) was born on his parents' farm in Great Bedwyn and became an English doctor who played a part in the history of anatomy, neorology and psychiatry. He was a founding member of the Royal Society. Medical students are taught that the arterial blood supply to the brain is called "The Circle of Willis."

Great Wishford

Bread Stones (SU 081 355)

The Bread Stones are situated in Great Wishford on the perimeter wall of the churchyard. They chronicle the price of bread from the Napoleonic wars to the present day. There is an official leaflet available inside the church.

The first stone records the price at an expensive 3 shillings and 4 pence per gallon in 1800. The second stone records a date of 1801, but was probably 1811 as the original stone was defaced before it was replaced by a local mason. If the date was considered to be 1811, I am unclear why it wasn't carved as that date. At the turn of the eighteenth century into the nineteenth, the country was blockaded by the French and imported wheat wasn't readily available and prices boomed. Great Wishford was hard hit and had to pay 8 pence and 4 pence more than Newbury and Winchester respectively. By 1812 the blockade had ended and the price fell. Over 100 years later the bread price had significantly dropped from the high in the early nineteenth century to only 10 pence per gallon, presumably because there was a much improved transportation supply chain and farming methods to reap the harvest were becoming more mechanised.

In order to justify the price and reassure the population, the price of bread was posted often in the churchyard or adjacent to it – the church being a place of congregation, where most inhabitants would see it. This was recorded in stone and was a widespread practice in the early 1800s. However, the Great Wishford Bread Stones are the only ones set close together for comparison and possibly the only ones to have survived. The practice continues to this day, the last stone to be placed was at the Millennium and records the price at £3.72 per gallon. Of course the stones engraved prior to 1971 are in pounds, shillings and pence and those thereafter are in our present day decimal currency – let us hope they don't change to be

Top: *The Bread Stones at Great Wishford.*

Above: *The people of Great Wishford march to Salisbury Cathedral to assert their rights.*

in Euros in the future!

The stones visible today are modern twentieth-century replacements, the originals having become barely legible, which is probably the reason that others haven't survived elsewhere. New stones are added at the time of significant events in the nation's history.

It seems odd that the price of bread should be recorded in gallons. In this context a gallon represents a dry volume of ingredients. There were ingredients for four quartern loaves to a gallon, which is about 2lbs. in weight for each loaf; this according to the Great Wishford website. The dictionary definition of a quartern loaf is one that weighs 4lbs. This is of course at odds with four quartern loaves per gallon – better to have used weight for the comparison and then avoided 215 years of confusion!

Grovely Charter (SU 079 354)

A commemorative stone is placed in the village to recognise the Charter of the Forest of Grovely 1603 - 2003. "Unity is Strength". The stone was placed by the Oak Apple Club of Great Wishford to celebrate 400 years of the charter. The villagers' rights to fuel goes

The Forest of Grovely Charter commemoration stone.

The Bishop Wordsworth Stone on Harnham Hill above Salisbury.

along the path.

Bishop John Wordsworth (1843 - 1911) at his own expense set about building a school on ground he purchased next to the Bishop's Palace in 1889. His school opened later in 1890 and was known as Bishop's School. In 1912, after his death, it became Bishop Wordsworth's School.

There is a blue plaque on the entrance to the school in the Cathedral Close commemorating the author William Golding, who was a teacher there.

Harnham Mill (SU 135 294)

Harnham Mill is situated on the River Nadder, feeding into the Avon at Salisbury. The mill building dates back to 1135 and was converted in 1550 to Wiltshire's first paper mill when the river was diverted under the building. Prior to this it was used for ecclesiastical purposes. It is thought that muniments (title deeds and documents relating to ownership of assets) from Sarum were stored here during the building of the new Cathedral.

The mill is built with Chilmark stone, some dating from c. 1200. It bridges the river by three branches, a mill race, eel stage and a head race vent. There are quatre foil windows in the end walls dating from c. 1250 and the upper storey brickwork dates from 1559.

The large pool in front of the mill is mostly shallow and a haven for ducks. The path in front of the mill turns sharply left at the end of the mill, proceeds across a weir and forms an attractive walk through the water meadows, with excellent views of Salisbury Cathedral, to Elizabeth Gardens in the city.

back much earlier than 1603, but the charter of that date confirms their rights.

On Oak Apple Day, which falls on 29 May each year, the village celebrates the right to collect wood from Grovely Forest on the hills above Great Wishford. The day starts with a loud band patrolling the streets waking everyone up. At sunrise the villagers walk to Grovely Wood and gather oak branches as a symbol of their privilege. This is followed by breakfast in the Royal Oak public house. The villagers' rights are emphasised by dancing in front of Salisbury Cathedral and claiming their rights inside the edifice by shouting "Grovely, Grovely and all Grovely". Another "Grovely" may be added for luck! Following this, celebrations are ongoing in the village.

Harnham

Bishop Wordsworth Stone (SU 135 287)

This inscribed stone is placed beside a footpath running parallel with the contours of Harnham Hill above Salisbury. It commemorates that the walk and the adjacent slope were presented to the citizens of Salisbury by John Wordsworth D.D., Bishop of Salisbury between 1885 and 1911. There are wonderful views over Salisbury and the Cathedral further

Harnham Water Mil, now a restaurant, adjacent to the Town Path across the weir to Salisbury's Elizabeth Gardens.

Visit Heaven's Gate at different times of the year to experience an enchantment that changes with the seasons.

Heaven's Gate

Sculptures (ST 823 424)

The sculptures at Heaven's Gate are inspired by their surroundings and are positioned roughly in a semi circle with the principal point of interest, a faceted annulus overlooking the smaller worked stones. Various aspects on the stones can be created by viewing them through the ring at different angles – photographic dreaming!

Heaven's Gate is a viewpoint overlooking Longleat Park – probably the best viewpoint in Wiltshire, in my opinion. The stones and viewpoint can be accessed from a footpath from a free car park on the minor road between Horningsham and the Longleat entrance. Please respect the stones and their surroundings – there is a touch of mystery and magic here.

The sculptures were made by Paul Norris for a Longleat Millennium project. Paul worked the stones for two years whilst living on the estate. They are made of Cornish granite and all except the circular stone were cut and formed in the Cornish quarry at Mabe.

A plaque describes the stones and the spirit in which they were carved. Quoting from the plaque in Paul Norris' own words: "Longleat uplifts my spirit and I know it does many others that live and visit this part of Wiltshire. My idea was for the work to blend into the atmosphere of Longleat and to be part of its future. The sculptures are figurative in an animal way, but are as much to do with the landscape as with animals."

Highworth

Tympanum (SU 201 925)

This Norman tympanum was moved from the room over the porch of St Michael's church to the outside north wall of the vestry in 1862, but again removed and placed in its present position inside the church over the entrance in 1904. It seems that most of its life it has been protected from the elements, which explains its excellent and crisp condition.

It probably shows Samson and the lion surrounded by an arch of twining stem sprouting growth. Samson is forcing the lion's jaw wide open. Note the length of the lion's tail – the Norman sculptor had doubtless never seen a lion.

The St Michael's church tympanum in Highworth.

Above: *The remains of Holt Spa.*

Right: *The plaque dating the fame of the spa to 1720.*

Holt

Spa (ST 862 621)

The spa pump of Holt Spa is in a niche at the south end of the factory of John Sawtell and Company in an area called "The Midlands." It has a Latin inscription above two columns. In the niche are, in relief, an urn and plaque in marble, which records that Lady Lisle and Rev. James Lewis patronised the spring and made it famous. The "famous" comment referred to the fact that the medicinal qualities of the water had become recognised as water from Holt Spa, presumably promoted by Lady Lisle and the Reverend. The remains of the spa have probably been reset in their present position to preserve them.

A well at Holt was sunk in 1688 (eventually there was more than one well). The water was found to contain various minerals, which enabled the spring to be promoted as a spa in 1713. As the plaque proclaimed, the spa became well known for its alleged curative properties in 1720. The owner of the land was Lord of the Manor, Edward Lisle, presumably Lady Lisle's husband.

The founder of the spa, widow Grace Harding bottled the water and sent it to London in 1725. By 1731 Henry Eyre was master of Holt Well. The well continued in use until the early nineteenth century.

Horningsham

Congregational Chapel (ST 812 411)

There is a long tradition that the chapel at Horningsham dates from 1566 and was erected by Scottish workmen employed in the reconstruction of Longleat House, which is nearby.

However, it is Grade II listed and the listing gives a build date of c. 1700. There were modifications in 1754, 1816 and 1863; doubtless the cast iron plaque was added when the earlier modifications were made.

The original Longleat House was burnt down in 1567, a year after the chapel was supposed to have been built for the builders, so 1566 appears to be wishful thinking! The heritage listing for Longleat gives a date of 1568.

Spotlight on Inn and Pub Signs

It is said that the most prolific form of public art is the ubiquitous inn or pub sign. The hand painting of signs is a dying art as there is a trend to use computer generated images on synthetic materials and recently even on wood, which is quicker to produce, bearing in mind the image appears on both sides of the sign. It follows, therefore that printing two copies one after the other must be cheaper than a traditional painted sign. Once stored under the name of the public house the file can be reprinted in the future at comparatively little cost. However, no more to be said of this ease of manufacture and smooth photographic appearance, we concern ourselves with the quality of skilled brush work, hand-mixed colours, a textured brush stroke finish and the sign writer's skill of uniform lettering.

How did it all begin? We must turn back time to the Roman era when the Romans invaded Britain for the second time in AD 43 and slowly established rule over most of Britain until c. AD 410. Drinking wine from grapes was a common refreshment in their homeland and an attempt was made to grow vines in Britain to support imports from Rome, which met with only partial success. The climate in Britain did not lend itself to the consistent ripening of the grapes. In order to sell the wine to the population the Romans opened tabernae in their walled towns. (The word "tavern" is derived from the Latin "taberna".)

To advertise their products, vines were hung on poles outside the premises. In the event that vines were unavailable they were substituted by shrubs or a bush. No doubt the premises also sold beer and mead, which was brewed before the Romans invaded. The first ale house with a painted sign to advertise alcohol for sale may well have been called "The Bush". There are a number of Bush Inns in England, but I am unable to find an example in Wiltshire, the nearest being over the border in Hampshire.

In films set in early Medieval times "The Blue Boar" seems to be the meeting place for deeds of cunning and bravery to be planned. It is unclear why the wild boar roaming the medieval forests should be blue, but the name is still used today – the Blue Boar in the village of Aldbourne is an example and of course there is a Blue Boar Row in Salisbury, named after the inn of that name which stood on the site where Debenhams store now trades. However, travellers would probably have spent their nights in monasteries, where the monks would have created their own refreshment!

In 1393 King Richard II decreed that all premises selling alcoholic products, which by this time would have been mainly ale and mead, must carry an exterior sign to signify that the building was an inn or alehouse. This was primarily for his ale tasters to know where to fulfil their employment. The term public house was probably not used until the eighteenth century, although there are some sources that go back earlier than this.

After King Henry VIII broke from Rome many of the inns and pubs were named after Royalty to show support for the Crown. Thus the populace could drink at "The Crown", "The King's Head" or "The Queen's Head" which in effect gave the break from Rome their backing. Previous to this many names were allied to the Roman Catholic faith. Eventually the practice expanded into naming drinking houses after famous historical figures, often patriotic. Then the stagecoach came on the scene and inn names followed suit with "The Coach and Horses", or if the inn was a freight stop, "Wagon and Horses" would have been appropriate. The inns for coaches or wagons would have had a wide covered entrance to a courtyard to service the horses, to unload goods and allow passengers a refreshment stop.

The most popular inn names through time are "The Red Lion", a common heraldic device; "The Crown", for reasons explained earlier; "The Bell", a reminder of the close association of the church with brewing ale; "The Royal Oak", Charles II hiding from the Parli-

The Royal Oak in Corsham, a Wadworth public house. The swing sign was, no doubt, painted by inn sign artist Dave Young. The Royal Oak is named after the tree in which King Charles II reputedly hid after being chased by the Parliamentarians after the Battle of Worcester in 1651. The inn sign pictorially records the event in a nutshell with a slice of humour added.

Not a traditional swing sign but a low relief painted panel on the Coach and Horses in Salisbury.

amentarians in a tree; "The George and Dragon"; "The White Hart", emblem of Richard II; "The Swan"; "The White Horse" and others.

When King Richard II ruled that all inns and taverns must display a sign, I imagine he didn't declare what form this should take. The most cost-effective way of sign display is to affix one directly flat to the wall of the premises. No doubt many did this, but it would soon become obvious that travellers approaching a hostelry have the best chance of noticing it with signage facing the direction of travel. Obviously since an approach can be from the opposite direction, such a sign needed to be double sided. Thus it was placed on a bracket projecting from the building. Perhaps it was soon noticed that a rigid sign caught the wind and pulled the bracket from the wall – the simple step of hinging the sign to make it swing prevented this from happening.

So today most of the public houses and inns have a swing sign, some with an ornate metalwork bracket, which is either attached to the building or is freestanding in a frame attached to a post, called a pillory, after the punishment post. Pillory signs are often remote from the building in a car park or on a green when the pub is set back from the road. The uncommon arrangement of a beam sign is sometimes seen, which stretches

across the road supported on both sides by a post. There is an example of this at Enford in the Salisbury Avon Valley near Upavon. In the centre is a swing sign supported by a flat wall sign on the building itself.

Turning now to the artwork itself – the sign must show the artists and sign writer's skill of producing an appealing portrayal of the name of the premises. It should also show the subject in an historical context or theme and habitat if representing flora or fauna on the panel. Painting a flat panel is half the effort of a double sided swing sign, some with repeat images others with differing, but connected images.

The preferred material upon which to place the image is exterior grade hardwood or aluminium. If using wood, a high quality exterior plywood will minimise distortion in the harsh winter weather conditions and hot summer sunshine the signs can receive in their exposed environment.

The paints required need to withstand harsh weather extremes; exterior oil-based paints or exterior sign writer's enamels will give the best time-tested performance. The application of varnish to the finished sign is optional, but usually two coats of yacht varnish will suffice.

The preparation of the board to take the final hand-painted image is important to prevent peeling. A coat of primer suitable for the material of the panel being painted is essential, followed by one or two coats of undercoat, the colour of which will depend on the predominant pigments used in the image. We are then left with the most important part of the process: the skill of the artist in producing an image based upon artwork supplied or self drawn. It will probably take eight days to paint a double sided sign, which, hope-

The Swan at Enford in the Avon Valley has a beam sign. The welded iron work around the swing sign (inset) shows the skill of the blacksmith.

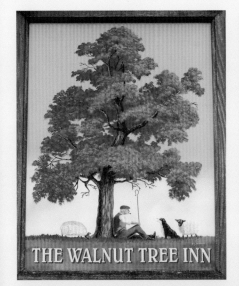

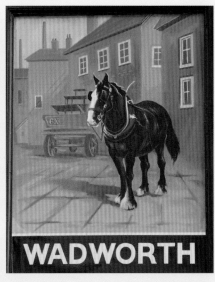

Above left and centre: *The Walnut Tree Inn is in Southbrook near Mere and the Wooden Spoon is in Downton, both are signed by J.P. Oldreive.* Left and above right: *Two signs on pillory posts, both Wadworths and painted by Dave Young – "The Black Horse" near the top of the Caen Hill canal lock flight in Devizes and "The Barge Inn" on the Kennet and Avon Canal at Seend Cleeve.*

Above: *The Milk Churn in Melksham, opened in July 2014, and won pub sign of the year in 2015. The sign depicts the area's dairy farming history and the added interest of a camouflaged Spitfire through the barn opening. The sign was painted by Phil Taylor who has painted a number of signs for Hall and Woodhouse. The reverse is a different scene on the milk churn theme, but painted by local artist Victor Steele.* Left: *The Glue Pot is in Swindon Railway Village. I assume the sign relates to the wood glue used in the manufacture of railway coaching stock in the railway works, long since closed.*

fully will last at least six years in a harsh environment and much more in better conditions.

A popular pastime when I was at school (many a long year ago!) was to record the names of pubs as we passed them on a journey. A particular game was the first person to spot a sign with four legs or someone's arms. One of the most prolific themes is based upon threes; "Three Bells", "Boars", "Cocks", "Crowns", "Horseshoes", "Kings", "Lions" and "Tuns", are just a few examples. Games like these are all the more difficult today bearing in mind the number of public house closures throughout the country. How often does one see "The Crown" or "The Wagon and Horses" boarded up?

I am glad to say that there is a society keeping an interest in inn and pub signs alive: the Inn Sign Society. Visit their website and it's a hive of information regarding the collation, history of the subjects portrayed, artists and their materials and the establishment of an archive for posterity. The society even hold an Inn Sign of the Year competition, which was won in 2014 by "The Milk Churn" in Melksham. A previous winner in Wiltshire was "The Poplars" in Wingfield, which won sign of the year in 2009. The sign shows a cricket match with polar trees as a backdrop, but now looks rather pitted and dirty, however viewed from a distance is still appealing.

A collage of Wiltshire pub signs. Clockwise: The Anchor and Hope in Salisbury, The Moonrakers in Pewsey, The Smoking Dog in Malmsbury, The Castle Hotel in Devizes, The Wheatsheaf in Lower Woodford and The Curriers Arms in Wootton Bassett.

Inglesham

Carving of Madonna and Child (SU 205 984)

This carving of Madonna and child has Saxon origins and appears to be part of a larger work. Above the figures is an inscription with "Maria" identifiable. In the top right there seems to be part of a hand pointing to the Christ child, if my interpretation is correct. This medium relief carving was at one time, before 1910, on the exterior south wall of the church. This can be confirmed by the scratch (mass) dial with a hole for the gnomon in the lower left of the artwork. This was a primitive form of sundial which, when the sun was out, gave worshipers the time to wait for mass.

The carving is inside St John the Baptist church in a remote spot in Inglesham, which is situated on a finger of Wiltshire probing into Gloucestershire. The church is close to the River Thames, known as Isis in its upper reaches. It is Grade I listed and is in the care of the Churches Conservation Trust, having been declared redundant and no longer used for worship. It is a significant church of the early thirteenth century with Saxon origins. The inside layout and décor is unexpected. The walls are covered in paintings and bible script from medieval to nineteenth-century work, albeit remnants. William Morris famed for his textile designs of the Arts and Crafts Movement, who lived just 10 miles away, oversaw restoration work in the nineteenth century to ensure the artistic substance and architecture of the church remained preserved.

Knook

Tympanum (ST 947 418)

A blocked doorway on the small church of St Margaret in Knook has a fine example of a tympanum. It has interlaced scrolls, which Pevsner calls "inhabited scrolls", with two symmetrical beasts each side of the tree of life.

There is much lichen covering the tympanum, which, although it makes it difficult to interpret, probably serves to protect it from the elements. Dating the tympanum is difficult, but is probably early Norman. Pevsner remarks about early eleventh-century motifs.

Liddington Castle

Millennium Commemoration (SU 209 797)
Liddington Castle is a univallate early Iron Age hill fort situated close to the Ridgeway long distance path. It dates from 700 - 500 BC. A commemorative plaque and topograph have been placed within the hill fort by the Parish Council to commemorate the Millennium, with support and help of the Ridgeway School, Ordnance Survey and English Heritage.

Liddington Castle was a favourite haunt of Richard Jefferies and Alfred Williams, both born not far from here. Liddington Castle is a one mile walk from the Swindon to Hungerford road via the Ridgeway and a permissive path to the hill fort. There is a view over Swindon and surrounding countryside.

and the lintel over the door, which shows three dogs and a huntsman trying to bring down a wild boar.

Lower Wadswick

Speke Monument (ST 843 674)
This monument is only accessible on foot as it is situated next to a stone wall on a footpath in the middle of fields. It is marked on the ordnance survey map with "Mon". It is very closely guarded by railings rendering the inscription very difficult to read. However, with perseverance it records the death of John Hanning Speke, whom I have previously mentioned as discoverer of the source of the Nile, with a memorial in Box church.

The monument reads: "Here the distinguished and enterprising African traveller Captain John Hanning Speke lost his life by accidental expression of his gun. September 15th 1864." He was out hunting with his gun and the position of the memorial suggests that it was placed on the exact spot where he met his demise.

Little Langford

Tympanum (SU 048 367)
Little Langford church is dedicated to St Nicholas of Mira, who has historically been associated with Santa Claus.

The tympanum is set in a Norman arch over the south door and dates prior to 1120. Featuring the likeness of a bishop with his right hand raised in blessing. His left hand holds a pastoral staff from which a branch has sprouted arching over his head. On the right of the tympanum are three birds on the top of tree branches.

The sprouting staff may represent the tree of life, which seems to appear on these early pieces of art work. It is also possible it represents the first miracle of St Aldhelm where his staff mushroomed while he was preaching. Note the zig-zag arch over the characters

Spotlight on Milestones and Turnpikes

Prior to getting into more depth on this subject, milestone is a generic term which includes mileposts mostly made of cast iron. Mile markers are an unconventional means of conveying distances and include, now scarce, AA enamel plates. A milestone is a reference point along a road from a fixed commencement point, usually from a recognisable landmark in a city or large town. They can either state distance travelled from a start point or mileage to a destination. The milestone may have Arabic or Roman numbering to indicate mileage. An Act of Parliament in 1593 created the statute mile equal to 1760 yards.

The Romans were the first to introduce milestones into Britain when they built paved roads to speed their army and transport movements. They measured their distances in Roman miles, which are shorter than the British mile. A Roman mile was 1000 double paces, i.e. right foot forward then followed through with the left foot – this represents a double pace, 1000 of them making a mile, which equates in distance to 1618 yards.

Roman milestones were cylindrical in shape. There are no Roman milestones remaining in Wiltshire, to my knowledge, but there is a good example near Hadrian's Wall at Vindolanda.

After the Romans left Britain in 410 AD most of the road system fell into ruin, but the Saxons did make use of the Roman's civil engineering work in Wessex. Subsequent to the Norman invasion the construction of paved highways did not resume in England until the early eighteenth century. Many of the Roman road remains that still existed were built over to create turnpikes.

There are many variations in style of milestone, both in shape and material used. Originally milestones were sculpted in stone with engraved letters and numbers, but as time progressed cast iron was popular, particularly subsequent to the industrial revolution. Stone and cast iron combination milestones are quite common, where the informative part of the marker is a cast iron plaque and the body sculpted out of stone or cast in concrete. The earliest dated milestone is in

Examples of stone milestones. Top, left to right: *Collingbourne Kingston, Hindon, near Cherhill on the A4, Whiteparish on the A27, Purton, and Little Frith near the A4.* Above, left to right: *Near Marlborough on the A4, Alderbury (Whaddon on the old A36), near Teffont, Knoyle Down on the A303 dated 1750, Avebury, and Marlborough on the A4.*

Examples of metal (principally cast iron) milestones and combination stones using cast plaques of iron. Damaged plaques that are replaced may well be of cast resin or non ferrous metal. The milestones are, in the top row, from left to right: *Donhead St Andrew on the A30, near Potterne Wick, Alderbury on the old A36, Tytherington dated 1840, between Hilperton and Trowbridge dated 1864 and Grittleton. Above, left to right: Trowbridge, near Warminster, Upavon, Mere, Airman's Corner (Stonehenge).*
At this latter location there were extensive road works in 2014 and the stone depicted must have been damaged, because it has been replaced with a replica. The final one is a metal plate only and is located in Yatton Keynell.

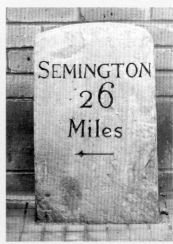

Above from left to right: *A private milestone showing the distance and direction to Tottenham House in Savernake Forest (SU 215 654); a National Cycle Network milestone in the Woodford Valley at Normanton; another National Cycle Network mile marker near Calne; a Wilts and Berks canal milestone in Swindon New Town.*

Left: *Two AA enamel plate markers used in villages from 1906 until 1939. They were originally introduced because local councils did not think it their responsibility. Until recently there was a circular enamel one on a wall of a garage in Shrewton. It has since been removed and its whereabouts are unknown.*

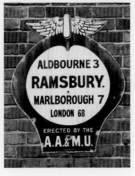

Oxfordshire (1696), and the earliest stone I have found in Wiltshire is 1750. There is a cast iron example in Tytherington dated 1840 and a combination milestone between Hilperton and Trowbridge dated 1864.

Individual milestones are marked on ordnance survey maps with a small dot and lettering "MS" and mileposts are logically marked "MP." In general milestones are found in a series of similar designs along stretches of road, but the design may change as the road passes through different old turnpikes or crosses county borders. There will be exceptions where an older stone is kept as part of a series. It is worth studying ordnance maps to find old drove roads, now abandoned routes which have been replaced by civil engineered roads, broadly going to the same destinations. Such old routes, now gravel and rutted green lanes, often have milestones tucked away on the verge; sometimes one has to part shrubbery to find them.

Milestone wording is frequently abbreviated, so Shaftesbury becomes Shaston, Southampton becomes Southton and Marlborough become Marlboro'. Even more unusual is the village of Christian Malford abbreviated to X. Malford and Pucklechurch to Puckle C.

There are milestones on canals, but in Wiltshire are scarce. However, there is one unusual example in the centre of Swindon New Town shopping centre, which gives the mileage to Semington on the Kennet and Avon Canal. The milepost was once adjacent to the Wilts and Berks Canal in Swindon on the waterway from Semington to Abingdon on the River Thames.

In recent years there has been a surge in cycling with old railway track beds taken over for the purpose, but also allowing ramblers to use them. The country is now interlaced with long distance cycle routes.

Through my locality is route 45 of the National Cycle Network linking Salisbury with Chester via Gloucester. Railways also have their mileage markers, but they are on the side of the permanent way, generally every quarter mile.

More unusual are private milestones – there is one to Tottenham House in Savernake Forest. Another less usual type is the stones set into pavements, which are not immediately obvious. Then there are the old AA wall discs with place identity and mileage to the nearest villages together with the mileage to London, and are quite scarce.

Turnpike trusts were introduced by Acts of Parliament from 1706 until the 1840s. Groups of local business-minded people formed bodies to create stretches of road between two centres with good hard wearing surfaces. For the use of the road, charges were levied depending on the cart, carriage or animals that were required to use it. This was termed a turnpike. The name is derived from the gate used to secure the stretch of highway, which resembled a row of secured pikes, spear-like weapons. When the gate was opened to allow passage the pikes were effectively turned. From 1767 milestones were compulsory on all turnpikes, but some stones are certainly dated prior to this ruling.

The Collins Lane Gate Toll House, now with the doorway of the toll booth walled up.

This is one of two pavement markers in Salisbury High Street One shows the mileage to Old Sarum (illustrated) and the other to Stonehenge.

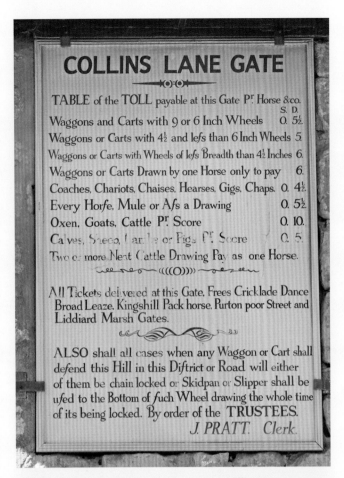

COLLINS LANE GATE

TABLE of the TOLL payable at this Gate Pr. Horse &co.

	S. D.
Waggons and Carts with 9 or 6 Inch Wheels	0. 5½.
Waggons or Carts with 4½ and lefs than 6 Inch Wheels	5.
Waggons or Carts with Wheels of lefs Breadth than 4½ Inches	6.
Waggons or Carts Drawn by one Horse only to pay	6.
Coaches, Chariots, Chaises, Hearses, Gigs, Chaps.	0. 4½.
Every Horfe, Mule or Afs a Drawing	0. 5½.
Oxen, Goats, Cattle Pr. Score	0. 10.
Calves, Sheep, Lambs or Pigs Pr. Score	0. 5.
Two or more Neat Cattle Drawing Pay as one Horse.	

All Tickets delivered at this Gate, Frees Cricklade Dance
Broad Leaze, Kingshill Pack horse, Purton poor Street and
Liddiard Marsh Gates.

ALSO shall all cases when any Waggon or Cart shall
defend this Hill in this Diftrict or Road will either
of them be chain locked or Skidpan or Slipper shall be
ufed to the Bottom of fuch Wheel drawing the whole time
of its being locked. By order of the TRUSTEES.

J. PRATT. Clerk.

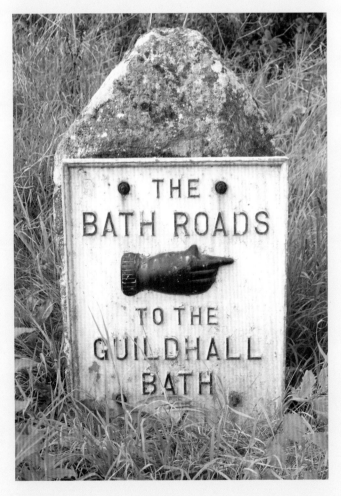

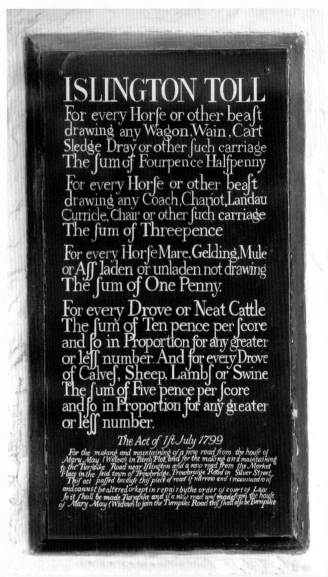

ISLINGTON TOLL

For every Horfe or other beaft
drawing any Wagon, Wain, Cart
Sledge Dray or other fuch carriage
The fum of Fourpence Halfpenny

For every Horfe or other beaft
drawing any Coach, Chariot, Landau
Curricle, Chair or other fuch carriage
The fum of Threepence

For every Horfe Mare, Gelding, Mule
or Afs laden or unladen not drawing
The fum of One Penny.

For every Drove or Neat Cattle
The fum of Ten pence per fcore
and fo in Proportion for any greater
or lefs number. And for every Drove
of Calves, Sheep, Lambs or Swine
The fum of Five pence per fcore
and fo in Proportion for any greater
or lefs number.

The Act of 1ft July 1799

For the making and maintaining of a new road from the houfe of
Mary May (Widow) in Birch Plot and for the making and maintaining
to the Turnpike Road near Iflington and a new road from the Market
Place in the faid town of Trowbridge, Trowbridge Road in Silver Street.
Thif act paffed becaufe thif piece of road if narrow and inconvenient if
and cannot be altered or kept in repair by the order of court of Law
fo it fhall be made Turnpike and if a new road waf made from the houfe
of Mary May (Widow) to join the Turnpike Road thif fhall also be Turnpike

Wiltshire Council

SEMINGTON TURNPIKE

Top left: *Collins Lane Gate Toll House charge board in Purton (SU 095 879).*

Top right: *The Islington Toll Board in Trowbridge (ST 858 586).*

Left: *The Bath Roads Turnpike Trust used squat milestones with a cast iron plate attached. The plates all directed the traveller to the Guildhall in Bath. This example is at the 5 Way Cross Roads south of Box (ST 839 671).*

Above right: *A small settlement has been built on the Seend to Trowbridge road called Semington Turnpike (ST 896 601).*

Maiden Bradley

Water Fountain (ST 802 390)

This is a substantial water fountain erected by Algernon 14th Duke of Somerset in 1891. An engraved plaque in rhyme states: "Drink travellers. Drink of Bradley's purest rill, which strange to say runs quite a mile up hill. Then to your panting steeds let all attend. An honest horse is surely man's best friend."

There is no water present today. Clearly it was designed as a water fountain and horse drinking trough, although the trough appears to be in marble and may have been replaced at some point. The rhyme states that the water has flowed uphill for a mile. This could mean that it has risen from the water table a distance away via a pipe or that it has been pumped to the fountain. A rill is a small brook and whatever the water source it appears to have been capped.

Water was supplied to the village by the Bradley estate in 1896 – the fountain was supplying water five years earlier according to the dedication.

Top: *Maiden Bradley water fountain and trough.*

Above: *At one time water spouted from the fox's mouth.*

Malmesbury

Monk in Meditation (ST 934 872)

In May 2014 at the corner of Oxford Street in Malmesbury, a statue of a seated monk was unveiled to the public. The statue, made of bronze resin, was sculpted by William R. Lazard, who is known for his sitting Cistercian Monk in Abbey House Gardens. The statue was donated to the Town Council by a local family.

Other works by William Lazard on public display are within the grounds of a school in Cwmamman in South Wales, in a cemetery in East Grinstead, for a church in Lingfield and Our Lady of Lourdes church in Hampton Court.

It is entirely appropriate for a meditating monk to be seated in the centre of Malmesbury considering the town's important twelfth-century former Benedictine abbey, which is situated in a dominant position overlooking the town. Next to the abbey are Abbey House Gardens – a not to be missed venue for any visitor to Malmesbury (an entrance fee is payable, which at tulip time in spring will certainly not be regretted). As mentioned earlier it is here that Lazard's other monk is seated amongst the tulips.

Monk in Meditation by William R. Lazard – 2014.

Hannah Twynnoy (ST 932 872)

Hannah Twynnoy was a thirty-three year old barmaid in the White Lion public House in Malmesbury.   A travelling menagerie of wild animals was put on display in the yard of the White Lion in 1703. One of the animals was a tiger, presumably in a barred cage. Hannah Twynnoy could not resist teasing the animal, despite warnings from the keeper that that the animal was dangerous. Eventually the tiger had enough of being taunted and somehow managed to maul the girl until she was dead.

The recorded tale states that the enraged animal pulled out the gate staple and escaped the cage and ripped her to pieces. Perhaps the staple wasn't secure and the tiger shook it loose or the bars of the cage were too far apart allowing the tiger to reach through – how it actually happened is a matter of conjecture, but the result was death.

The gravestone of Hannah Twynnoy in the abbey churchyard. Hannah could not have afforded such a stone as this, neither to be placed at rest in the abbey grounds. So who financed this memorial and the funeral? Did she have a fling with a well-to-do man frequenting the pub. Perhaps the event was so memorable it merely deserved recognition by a poetic mason – who knows?

A gravestone in the abbey churchyard records an epitaph:

"In bloom of life
She's snatched from hence,
She had not room
To make defence;
For Tyger fierce
Took life away.
And here she lies
In a bed of Clay
Until the Resurrection Day."

On the 300th anniversary of her death in 2003, every schoolgirl under eleven in Malmesbury named Hannah placed a flower on her grave.

Site of South Gate (ST 934 869)

The site of Malmesbury town's South Gate is marked with a narrow rectangular bronze plaque in the pavement, as are the positions of the other town gates. There is also a quotation from Sir John Betjeman:
"Malmesbury has stayed the same size, growing neither bigger nor smaller. The arched gateways by which you used to enter it by road have disappeared, but it is still surrounded by a skirt of cottages whose gardens go down to the river."

Defensive walls and entrances to a settlement at Malmesbury have existed since the Iron Age, starting with wooden palisades and followed by stone. In 1136-9 Bishop Roger of Salisbury rebuilt the town walls. Leland noted four main gates to access the town in the sixteenth century, which were ruinous, South, East, West and Postern, but there may have been a fifth. Defences were strengthened during the Civil War, but much was slighted after the war, probably as early as 1646.

Abbey Entrance Detail (ST 933 874)

There is no doubt that the twelfth-century entrance to Malmesbury Abbey is a work of art. The recessed arched entrance is a feast of Norman carvings depicting beasts, biblical figures showing stories from the bible and geometric patterns. There are eight separate connected arches, which Pevsner calls "orders", with the geometric orders separating bible scenes and figures. The ornamentation is surrounded on the outside of the abbey by a plain outer arch which perfectly sets off the inner.

Within the inner entrance arch is a porch with sculptures showing the twelve apostles. There a six seated apostles on each side of the porch with a horizontal flying angel over their heads. Over the inner door is a tympanum showing Christ held by two angels.

In the cloisters at the rear of the abbey a column has been constructed showing ornamental sculptural remnants from the ruined part of the abbey.

High Relief of St Aldhelm (ST 934 872)

On the outside wall of the catholic church of St Aldhelm is a high relief wall sculpture of St. Aldhelm set against,

Above: *Six of the Twelve apostles in the porch of Malmesbury Abbey.*

Far left: *The magnificent Norman doorway on the south face of the abbey.*

Left: *Detail from the intricate carving surrounding the entrance.*

Below: *Southgate plaque.*

"MALMESBURY HAS STAYED THE SAME SIZE, GROWING NEITHER MUCH BIGGER NOR SMALLER. THE ARCHED GATEWAYS BY WHICH YOU USED TO ENTER IT BY ROAD HAVE DISAPPEARED, BUT IT IS STILL SURROUNDED BY A SKIRT OF COTTAGES WHOSE GARDENS GO DOWN TO THE RIVER."
Sir John Betjeman on Malmesbury

THIS PLAQUE MARKS THE SITE OF THE OLD
SOUTH·GATE
OF MALMESBURY.

what I believe to be, a depiction of his original monastery church founded in 676 AD. Underneath his person on the sculpture are the following words:

"St. Aldhelm 639 - 709, Abbot of Malmesbury and Bishop of Sherborne, Latin poet and ecclesiastical writer."

Left: *A masonry column in the cloisters with architectural details from the parts of Malmesbury Abbey no longer standing.*

Below: *The high relief sculpture of St Aldhelm on the outside wall of the Catholic church of St Aldhelm in Malmesbury.*

Top right: *Marlborough Jubilee Clock.*

Right: *School Commemoration Stone.*

Marlborough

Jubilee Clock (SU 187 691)

The Jubilee Clock was placed in Marlborough High Street in 2002 to commemorate the Golden Jubilee of Queen Elizabeth II.

It was apparently news in 2003 that the clock was running slow – I suppose this is unacceptable with today's technology, particularly if we can reach and photograph a comet on time!

Secondary School Commemoration Stone (SU 188 697)

Standing at the edge of a large public green next to the road to Swindon from Marlborough is an engraved stone commemorating the site of Marlborough Secondary School, which stood on this site from 1946 until 1965.

The stone was erected by former staff and pupils of the school and was unveiled in 2000 by Canon Henry Pearson. Being at the start of a dog walking area, the dogs, unfortunately, show no respect for the stone or the teaching edifice it represents.

Melksham (Bowerhill)

Water Turbine (ST 916 616)
I am unsure why a steam turbine should be placed in this location, but suffice to say that it was placed by the Bowerhill Turbine Project under the direction of the West Wiltshire Industrial Archaeological Society. It was formerly at Kingston Mill at Bradford on Avon, a textiles factory.

A brushed metal plate defines the function of the turbine in words more adequate than I could describe and I quote:

"The turbine was built by Gilbert Gilkes & Co. Ltd., of Kendal, their order number 1381 of April 1900. It is a Francis type inward flow single vortex machine of 38HP which worked on a fall of 5ft. 3 inches utilising some 39,156 gallons of water per minute. It was designed to run at 34 RPM.

The machine was submerged, water entering through guide blades which could be regulated according to the power requirement. Driving the vanes of the internal 78 inch diameter 'runner' it discharged

Steam turbine formerly at Bradford on Avon.

Chafyn Grove Cross.

through the draught tube at the bottom of the machine. This, being partially immersed in the tail race, created a vacuum enabling effective use to be made of the full available head.

Power was transmitted by the vertical hollow shaft to a suspension bearing carried on the fixed spindle passing through the machine's axis. A further shaft connected with the crown wheel and bevel gearing to drive machinery, and later, a direct current electric generator. It remained operational until circa 1951, being erected here by individual effort with the assistance of local and national firms."

The plaques were unveiled by Dr Alex Moulton, OBE, RDI. Feng, The Hall, Bradford on Avon and Mr R.D. Taylor, Gilbert Gilkes and Gordon Ltd., Kendal, on 29 September 1989.

Mere

Chafyn Grove Cross (ST 811 323)
This memorial cross is in the churchyard of St Michael's. It was erected in 1904 as a memorial to Julia Chafyn Grove, who died in 1891. It has a limestone base and sandstone shaft and is Grade II listed. The listing states that it is an example of a well-executed medieval cross used as a monument.

Julia Chafyn Grove lived in Zeals House, a mansion standing in a walled park near Mere. In 1695 William Chafyn was Sherriff of Wiltshire and his daughter married John, son of Hugh Grove. The descendants of this family lived in Zeals House until 1968.

Julia was the first benefactress of a school in Salisbury and in 1916 it was renamed Chafyn Grove School after her. She also endowed a ward at Salisbury Hospital.

William Lander (ST 811 324)
The plaque commemorating William Lander (1763 - 1843), who lived in Mere, is situated on the front of a house, once his residence, in Castle Street. There is a

memorial to Lander in the churchyard of St Michael's in Mere.

He was a musical instrument maker and inventor. One of his notable inventions was a road measuring wheel called a "Waywiser." It measured distance in links, chains and furlongs. An example of his measuring wheel is held by the Salisbury and South Wilts Museum. Other inventions included musical horns, a teeth extracting instrument and water pumping equipment.

Dolling Monument (ST 812 323)

Near St Michael's churchyard gate there is a headstone recording the fate of Edward Dolling, who died of smallpox. He did not contract the disease from the normal infection route, but by experimenting with inoculation. He injected himself with smallpox serum in 1737 and died as a result at the young age of twenty-one.

Dolling's attempt at inoculation was nearly sixty years before Edward Jenner discovered a more certain method of combatting the disease using cowpox serum in 1796.

Clock Tower (ST 804 323)

The Clock Tower is the focus of the square in Mere. It was built in 1868 and paid for by Albert Edward, Prince of Wales, in 1901 to become Edward VII. The Prince of Wales' feathers are on a tablet on the structure. The clock replaced a medieval two-storey Market House, which was becoming dilapidated.

In the cross loft of the Market House in 1823, William Barnes a local poet and schoolmaster opened his first school. There is a slate engraved plaque commemorating this event in a lancet window space on the body of the tower.

Milton Lilbourne

George Carter (SU 190 605)

A very large headstone in Milton Lilbourne St Peter's churchyard is dedicated to George Carter, the great huntsman, also of his wife. He was born at Bromfield in Shropshire on 29 November 1792 and died at Milton on 21 November 1884.

Above: *Mere Clock Tower.*

Left: *William Barnes commemoration remembering the school in the cross loft of the old Market House.*

Below: *The Prince of Wales' feathers dated 1868.*

His headstone records that he carried the horn with The Oakley; Hon. Grantley Berkeley, from 1831 to 1833. His Grace the Duke of Grafton, Whittlebury Forest, from 1833 to 1842. The Tedworth; Mr Thomas Assheton Smith, from 1842 to 1865.

A book was written on his life by I.H.G. in 1885 called *Hound and Horn*.

George Carter's headstone.   *Jubilee Postbox.*

Jubilee Postbox (SU 189 609)

Near the main Pewsey road is a commemorative postbox in a brick pillar with a brass plate celebrating the Golden Jubilee of the accession to the throne of Queen Elizabeth II.

At one time the Post Office started painting the cyphers on their boxes with gold paint. This significantly enhanced them, but the practice now seems to have stopped.

Old Sarum

Crop Circle (SU 139 331)

Crop circles are Wiltshire phenomena. This example was seen in spring viewed from Old Sarum. It is unusual for a crop circle to be in a field of rape, they are normally created in a ripe cornfield, probably much to the annoyance of the farmer. They are always the subject of speculation, but I am sure they are all man-made in the dead of night – unless you know otherwise. They are invariably based on circles, which are geometrically easy to produce with a central stake, a length of string or rope and flat boards attached to feet to trample around the central point. Move the stake within the circle and more intricate patterns begin to form.

The reader will have to search their own crop circles out, as obviously the one depicted was removed with the harvest.

Ordnance Survey Triangulation Commemoration Stone (SU 142 329)

Below Old Sarum earthworks and castle, adjacent to the Salisbury to Amesbury road, is situated an inscribed stone commemorating the base line for the start of the triangulation of Britain in 1794. The script on the stone is in an unusual font and is in some lighting conditions is very difficult to interpret. The wording is:

"In 1794 a line from this site to Beacon Hill was measured by Captain W. Mudge of the Ordnance Survey as a base for the triangulation of Great Britain. Presented by Master Masons in 1967."

Above the stone on the ramparts of Old Sarum is a plaque commemorating William Mudge.

Above: *The commemoration stone at the side of the road below Old Sarum.*
Top right: *The triangulation pillar on the top of Win Green Hill near the Wiltshire border with Dorset. Trigg pillars are painted white to aid observation (ST 925 207)*
Right: *The theodolite mounting plate on top of the triangulation pillar.*

Supporting the commemoration stone is a plaque on the ramparts of Old Sarum commemorating Lieutenant Mudge's base line for the start of the triangulation. It is noted that William Mudge's rank is Captain on the stone and Lieutenant on the plaque. As far as I can determine William Mudge left the service as a Lieutenant. Is it possible that Captain Zachary Mudge, who was engaged in coastal survey work around the same time, has been confused with Lieutenant William Mudge?

In a field adjacent to the commemoration is embedded vertically in the ground a cannon barrel. On the relevant ordnance survey map the position is recorded as "Gun End of Base". This was used as a positive location for the start of the base line to Beacon Hill, which I believe to be in Bulford. William Mudge's base line is 36,574 feet (11,253 metres) long. From each end of this line a huge theodolite made by Jessie Ramsden in 1791 was used to plot the position of distant places by triangulation. This process was eventually repeated all over Great Britain.

Today when out on a hilly walk we often come across a white pillar on the high point on a hill, these are called trig pillars and are the triangulation points from which positions of other distant points can be measured. 6500 of the white pillars, usually made of concrete, were placed during the re-triangulation of Great Britain which started in 1936. The re-triangulation work lasted until 1962. Many of the pillars are no longer used, but there are still 5500 in existence and are valuable position locaters for walkers in the hills, moorland and wild places. Of course on an expanse of lower lying ground trig pillars are still necessary, but they are more difficult to find. GPS now tells us exactly where we are and, with a satellite navigation aid in a motor vehicle, how far we have to go to reach our destination and in what direction we are travelling.

Each pillar has a theodolite mounting plate on its flat top surface. The theodolite was levelled and angles measured from the pillar to other distant points. Another pillar would be used in another visible location and the angles measured to the same distant points. Their location could then be accurately determined. Geometry allows the distance to be calculated from point to point. The triangulation pillar pictured also has a flush bracket and a GPS network plaque attached and states that it is part of this modern network.

The Parliament Tree   (SU 138 321)

The sarsen stone commemorating the Parliament Tree and William Pitt is situated below Old Sarum Castle at the side of a footpath known as The Portway. The actual site of the Parliament Tree is a little to the north of the sarsen stone in the middle of a field. The tree was an elm and has long since disappeared. A sapling elm was planted by Robert Key M.P. on 7 June 2000 following collaboration between English Heritage, Ordnance

Survey, Salisbury District Council and Wiltshire Wildlife Trust. I suppose this was partly to establish the precise location of the old elm. I have to say that an elm tree will have little chance of survival with Dutch elm disease prevalent in this country, unless a disease resistant variety has been planted.

The plate on the stone has clearly been replaced as the recess the plate sits in is a different shape. I do personally remember seeing the old plate and subsequently an empty space, presumably due to vandalism.

As the Saxon Gate bronze axe ages it is taking on a striking patina.

The plaque reads: "This stone erected by the Corporation of New Sarum commemorates that near this spot, beneath the spreading branches of an elm tree, members of Parliament for the Borough of Old Sarum were in former times elected, most notable of whom was William Pitt, afterwards Earl of Chatham, who forged those links of Empire which now bind our fellow citizens beyond the seas in affection to the mother country. Wherefore let this place be for ever enshrined in the hearts of our countrymen."

Old Sarum was a Parliamentary constituency until the Reform Bill of 1832. The site was used until this date to elect members of Parliament in a temporary booth underneath the elm tree, which was on the boundary of the former Old Sarum. Old Sarum was a "Rotten Borough," a constituency with only a small number of men eligible to vote giving rise to, perhaps, very predictable results.

Saxon Gate – Axe (SU 149 333)

This Bronze Age axe, actually made in bronze, is situated in the centre of a roundabout at Saxon Gate. Old Sarum airfield is on the right and a new housing complex is on the left (proceeding onward to the east from the roundabout).

The work was commissioned by Persimmon Homes from Angela Cockayne, who has included the GPS reading of the site location on the sculpture.

Her other public works of art include "Tide Clock" and "Hour Glass" in Bath and a number of artworks at Street in Somerset for Clarks shoe company. Her website shows her other works of art.

Airfield Artwork (SU 153 334)

This stainless steel artwork is situated in the viewing compound at Old Sarum airfield. The title of the work is not mentioned on the artwork, but it was placed to commemorate 100 years of aviation between 1903 and 2003. The latter being the date it was unveiled.

It was designed by Terrence Clark and made by Terrence and Becca Clark, who are artists and blacksmiths. The work has the appearance of a vertical Concorde with two rods pointing to the heavens, possibly indicating the future of aviation in space flight.

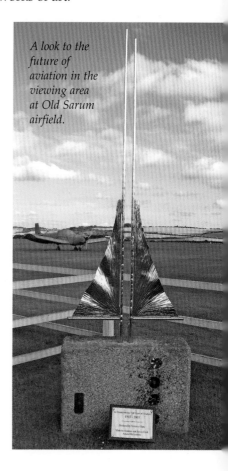

A look to the future of aviation in the viewing area at Old Sarum airfield.

Pewsey

King Alfred (SU 164 601)

Inscriptions on the plinth of the statue to King Alfred the Great (849 - 901) read: "This statue of his most illustrious ancestor is erected to commemorate the Coronation of His Majesty King George V, June 22nd 1911. A King who grandly follows in King Alfred's footsteps." A second panel praises Alfred: "It was his a sinking nation's fame to save, to foster, latent worth and patriot zeal and build on virtues based a nations weal." A third panel also commemorates Alfred: "Once a chief landowner in this vale (Vale of Pewsey), King Alfred fought nobly for his country's benefit."

The statue was erected on June 23rd 1913.

King Alfred famously routed the Danes at the Battle of Ethandun in 878, which will be dealt with more fully in another *Intriguing Wiltshire* series volume.

The statue of King Alfred the Great in the centre of Pewsey.

Purton

The Maskelyne Memorials (SU 097 872)

Nevil Maskelyne was Astronomer Royal between 1765 and 1811 when he died. The tomb has a brass plaque with words by the Purton Historical Society. The information on the plaque is concise and to the point, so I will quote from the plaque :

"Nevil Maskelyne DD FRS Astronomer Royal 1765 - 1811. Born in Kensington 5th October 1732, third son of Edmund Maskelyne of Purton. Died at Greenwich 9th February 1811 and interred in St. Mary's Churchyard on 20th February.

Educated at Westminster School and Trinity College, Cambridge.   Ordained 1755,   MA (Cantab) 1757, DD1777.   Elected Fellow of the Royal Society 1758. Took part in scientific expeditions to St. Helena and Barbados 1761 - 1763 on behalf of the Royal Society.

The grave of Nevil Maskelyne, Astronomer Royal 1765 - 1811.

Appointed Astronomer Royal by King George III in 1765. Served at the Royal Observatory, Greenwich, for 46 years until his death.   Became internationally renowned for his astronomical discoveries and for the publication of the Nautical Almanac which enabled mariners to determine their position accurately. This work established Greenwich as the location of the Prime Meridian.

Awarded the Copley Medal 1775. Elected a Fellow of the American Academy of Arts and Science 1788. Elected to the Institut National des Sciences et des Arts (Paris) 1802.

Funded by a Community Arts Grant from Wiltshire Council. Purton Historical Society 2011."

The title Astronomer Royal is an honour bestowed on a renowned scientist working in the field of Astronomy. There is a subsidiary post to the Astronomer Royal, that of the Astronomer Royal for Scotland, first appointed in 1834.

Charles II founded the Royal Observatory at Greenwich in 1675 and appointed the first person to fill the post of Astronomer Royal, John Flamsteed, whose

Purton Stoke

Salts Hole or Spa (SU 085 906)

West of the village of Purton Stoke along a lane crossing a common can be found a small building covering a spring. The spring is marked on the ordnance survey map as a Salts Hole and is more commonly known as Purton Spa. Indeed the metal gate advertises the fact.

The spring had for many centuries been used for fresh water by the locals and some of those with ailments noticed an improvement in their well-being. However, in bad winters the surrounding land used to flood causing problems over the years for the landowners. In the 1850s Dr Samuel Sadler was the landowner and he is alleged to have drained the area, moved in soil to surround the site and placed railings around the earthwork to prevent access. However, the locals broke into the compound and continued to access the spring water.

There is also a story that tells of an illness contracted by Dr Sadler that caused him to try the waters himself. Upon an improvement in his well-being he decided to erect a pump house over the spring in 1859 and sell the water as a commercial enterprise. He arranged for a Dr Voelcker to make a full analysis of the water to determine any medicinal benefits. Above the door of the pump house is inscribed the following:

"This ancient Salts-Hole. Sulphated and bromo-iodated saline water. Analyzed by D. Voelcker 1860.

The Celtic cross memorial for Mervin Story Maskelyne.

The Spa is easily accessible from Stoke Common Lane in Purton Stoke.

claim to fame was the first sighting of Uranus. In 1720 George I appointed Edmund Halley Astronomer Royal, who is renowned for predicting the return of a comet, with which we are all familiar as Halley's Comet.

The Celtic cross memorial has inscriptions on three sides of its base, of which the principal dedication is difficult to interpret due to lichen growth. However, I hope I have the deciphered it correctly. It reads:

"To the honoured memory of Mervin Nevil Story Maskelyne DSc FRSDL. Born Sept. 3rd 1823, died May 20th 1911. Eldest son of Anthony and Margaret Story Maskelyne of Basset Down and Purton. MP for the Cricklade Division of Wiltshire."   The memorial continues on to record the memory of his wife.

The remaining two inscriptions read:

"Keeper of the mineral department of the British Museum."

"Professor of Mineralogy, University of Oxford, Hon. Fellow of Wadham College."

The Maskelyne memorials are next to the south wall of St Mary's church. The churchyard also contains the remains of an ancient preaching cross, with some of the shaft and base damaged over time.

The inscription above the door of the Spa is confused by dappled sunlight.

Whatever the reason, supposed illness or not, which caused Dr Sadler to venture into the business of selling spa water, it became successful. In 1921 the Spa was purchased by Sergeant Fred Neville after he had left the army and continued to sell the bottled spring water. The water was sold at eight pence a bottle far afield from Purton Stoke. At the onset of the Second World War petrol rationing caused delivery problems and the water was only available locally. Sales continued until 1952. It is said that the introduction of the NHS in 1948 caused the death knell to sound for the business.

Rabley

The Venus of Calne (SU 204 707)

This buxom statue is in the car park of Rabley Arts Centre near Mildenhall. It is sculpted by Richard Cowdy of Calne, who earlier in the Gazetteer has a number of public works of art highlighted.

The Venus of Calne, was so named by Richard Cowdy because it is based upon the Willendorf Venus, a fertility doll believed to date from the Palaeolithic age. The fertility doll was discovered in Austria by an

archaeologist in 1908. Richard Cowdy has used the fertility doll figure for a number of his sculptures, one of which reclines and another which he calls an energised version with her arms and one leg in the air.

There are other sculptures around the building, one of which appears to be waves in motion.

Royal Wootton Bassett

Fundamental Motherhood (SU 068 825)

The statue of Fundamental Motherhood is on Station Road a short distance from   the High Street of Royal Wootton Bassett. It was sculpted in stone by D. Lansdown Esquire and presented to the town by him in September 1967.

Top: *Fundamental Motherhood.*
Above: *Two Jubilee Commemorations?*

Jubilee Stone (SU 074 836)

Some confusion here. The unweathered stone was photographed shortly after installation for the Queen's Golden Jubilee in 2002 and donated by Wootton Bassett Town Council. The crooked weathered stone was photographed more recently and has clearly been knocked. It was donated by David and Stella Taylor and Family. Two Jubilee Stones?

Salisbury

The Walking Madonna (SU 143 296)

The Walking Madonna is situated on the Cathedral Close lawn and is passed walking from the High Street to the Cathedral west front. The sculpture was cast in bronze by Dame Elisabeth Frink in 1981.

Dame Elizabeth Frink was born in Suffolk in 1930 and died in 1993. She was well known for her human form and horse sculptures. Her method of producing sculpture was based upon placing wet plaster over a wire armature, approximately the size and outline of the subject in mind. Once the armature had received a sufficient thickness of plaster it was fettled and carved to the detail required. The finished plaster model was used to create a mould from which the bronze casting was made.

There is more than one Walking Madonna in existence for Dame Elizabeth was known to have cast up to four of her subjects from one mould. There is known to be another casting in the grounds of Chatsworth House in Derbyshire.

Cloaked Figure IX (SU 142 295)

Another sculpture is on permanent display on the Cathedral Close lawn near the west front titled Cloaked Figure IX. It is sculpted in bronze by Lynn Chadwick (1914 - 2003). The female figure gives the impression of slowly and gracefully moving towards the west front of the Cathedral with her cloak gently brushing the floor in her wake.

The sculpture is one of a series of walking, standing and seated figures created in the 1970s at the height of his career. The figure is on long term loan from the Osborne Samuel Gallery in London and was significantly placed on the Close Green in the centenary year of Lynn Chadwick's birth.

Lynn was trained as a draughtsman in a number of architect's offices. His initial foray into artistic creation was with mobiles (artworks that move in the wind), but turned to static sculpture at the time of the Festival of Britain in 1951, when his sculpture "The Fisheater" was exhibited at the Tate Gallery in that year. In 1956 he won the International Sculpture Prize at the Venice Biennale and in 1964 was awarded a CBE.

The Walking Madonna is facing away from Salisbury Cathedral and appears to be walking towards the city centre.

Cloaked Figure IX in front of Salisbury Cathedral. Its title suggests there are eight other cloaked figures in existence

Henry Fawcett Statue (SU 144 300)

The statue of Henry Fawcett stands facing Blue Boar Row on the northern edge of the Market Place in the centre of Salisbury. It was sculpted by Richard Henry Hope-Pinker and erected in 1887.

A plaque on the plinth placed by Salisbury District Council and Salisbury Civic Society gives a potted life story: "Born in Salisbury in 1833. Blinded in a shooting accident, he became Professor of Political Economy at Cambridge University and a Liberal MP. He campaigned for equal political rights for women and married Millicent Garrett.

Appointed Postmaster General in 1880 he reformed the Post Office by introducing the sixpenny telegram, tablets on letter boxes to show collection times, a savings scheme and postal orders. He introduced a parcel post service in 1883.

Millicent became the president of the National Union of Women's Suffrage Societies and played a key role in persuading Parliament to give women the vote.

Henry Fawcett died in 1884."

A newspaper cutting found in my late father-in-law's possessions expands upon the shooting accident that blinded Henry Fawcett. His father suffered from an incipient cataract of one eye (probably his gun sighting eye). While shooting game on Harnham Hill, Salisbury, he took aim at a bird which had taken flight on the same trajectory as his son was standing. Henry took lead shot in both eyes, blinding him instantly. The description of his father having an incipient cataract suggests he may been unaware of his condition at the time of the accident

Sydney Herbert Statue (SU 142 313)

The statue of Sydney Herbert, 1st Baron Herbert of Lea, is tucked away in Victoria Park in Salisbury. It is unfortunately, shadowed by trees and is no longer in a prominent position, unlike its original location outside the Guildhall in the centre of Salisbury. It was moved in 1953, prior to the Coronation of Queen Elizabeth II, to provide an open space for civic and state occasions.

The sculptor was Baron Carlo Marochetti. He was born in Turin in Italy in 1805, but came to England for various commissions in 1848 and made the bronze statue of Herbert in 1863, five years before he died.

Herbert was born in Richmond in 1810. After an education at Harrow and a university placement at Oxford, he became MP for South Wiltshire in 1832. He

Henry Fawcett's statue in the Salisbury Market Place. It is not unknown after a city event or a rowdy revelling evening to find the statue adorned in a street cone, scarf or other decorations.

The statue of Sydney Herbert, Secretary of War during the Crimean conflict between 1853 and 1856.

eventually joined the cabinet as Secretary of War, both before and during the Crimean conflict. He sent his friend , Florence Nightingale, to the hospital at Scutari, where her nursing became legendary.

He died at Wilton House in 1861 (his father was the 11th Earl of Pembroke) and his grave is in the churchyard at Wilton.

Bas Relief (SU 144 303)

Walking towards the city centre on the left hand side of Castle Street one is confronted with this attractive young lady set into a wall facing your direction of travel. She is a bas relief sculpture of a lady who appears to have a hair style from the Regency period and no care in the world. Beyond this I have no information.

Gilbert of Salisbury
(Seasonal, 2014 location SU 145 300)

Gilbert may not be a sculpture, but he certainly is a horticultural work of art. In 2014 he was situated in front of the Guildhall in the summer months.

Right: Bas relief in Castle Street.

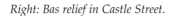

GILBERT OF SALISBURY by Deborah Hall

Gilbert lives
In the middle of town
On account of his size
He's easily found
At eight feet high
And five feet wide
He sits with a grin
To show off his pride
Everyone loves him
Cute as a bear
You can't help but smile
When seeing him there
With pointed tail
And wings out spread
Red and green
From toe to head
A creature of fancy
Made all of plants
When we are asleep
He's likely to dance
Floating like magic
His feet off the ground
From street to street
They move him around
Have you guessed what he is yet?
I'll give you a clue
The smoke from his nostrils
Is probably blue
Of course! He's a dragon
As everyone knows
The mystery is
Where next will he go

Salisbury City Council
01722 342860
info@salisburycitycouncil.gov.uk
www.salisburycitycouncil.gov.uk

On the railings in front of Gilbert was a plaque with a poem written by Deborah Hall.

Mural under Milford Street Bridge *(SU 148 299)*

The painted murals under Milford Street bridge are a wonderful and picturesque way of preventing graffiti from scarring the walls of the bridge carrying the city bypass over Milford Street. In the upper picture the Giant and his companion Hobnob make an open air appearance in front of the Guildhall during Silver Jubilee celebrations in 1977, but I have seen them recently at a St George's Day event in the Market Square. They are normally on display in the Salisbury and South Wilts Museum.

In the lower scene a drover or "cow walloper" has purchased cows in the cattle market in the Market Square (before it was moved out of town) and drives them up Milford Street to Milford goods station. One of his cows appears to have entered Foster's Bakery, which was situated on the corner of Milford Street and Guilder Lane. Foster's was the hub of the community with fresh bread and cakes made on the premises.

There are five scenes on the left hand wall under the bridge and nine points of interest or scenes on the right hand wall under the bridge.

Top: *Scene 2 on the left wall under the bridge shows the Salisbury Giant and Hobnob in front of the Guildhall.*
Above: *Scene 2 and 3 on the right wall under the bridge shows a drover and Foster's Bakery.*

The Giant and Hobnob at the head of a procession into the Market Square on St George's Day 2007.

The Giant's jesters in the Market Square. They mingle in the crowds of onlookers and make all the children very happy.

Mural of Stone Curlew (SU 141 299)

This mural of a stone curlew is on the rear wall of a toilet block at Harcourt car park in Salisbury.   The mural faces Elizabeth Gardens and seems to me to be a professional representation of the bird.   There is no signature of the artist (that I can find).   10% of our population of stone curlews can be found on Salisbury Plain, which is, no doubt, the reason this bird has been chosen to be represented in Salisbury.

Titanic Remembrance
(SU 147 293 - seat) (SU 149 299 - mural detail)

A simple bench seat and a silver birch tree in Churchill Gardens, Salisbury, hold the memory of Eileen and Neal McNamee, who lost their lives on R.M.S. *Titanic* on 15 April 1912.   A plaque on the bench reads:

"R.M.S. TITANIC   In memory of the young Salisbury couple, Eileen and Neal McNamee who perished on the R.M.S. *Titanic* on April 15th 1912."

Eileen is painted with her parasol on a large mural in Milford Street in the city. She was born in Plymouth in 1892. Neal McNamee was born in Ireland in 1884. He was working for Liptons the grocers in Silver Street, Salisbury, when he met his future wife Eileen O'Leary. Eileen's family moved from Plymouth to Salisbury, where Eileen went to school. After her education she joined Liptons in Silver Street as a cashier. Neal and Eileen fell in love and married on 17 January 1912.

At some point between Neal meeting Eileen and their marriage his job moved from the Salisbury branch of Liptons to the Bournemouth shop. Neal lived in Bournemouth and during the time he was working at his home town branch he was offered a position at Liptons in the USA. Neal must have been a hard-working and efficient employee to have been offered the move to America, which he accepted. I imagine Eileen would also have had the opportunity of employ-ment, as their passage was quickly arranged.

They boarded the *Titanic* at Southampton as third class passengers. The fate of the *Titanic* is well docu-mented. Both died in the ship's sinking – Neal was

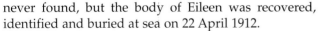

Above Left: *Churchill Gardens and a birch tree planted in memory of the McNamees*

Above: *Eileen McNamee painted within the large mural beneath Milford Street bridge.*

Left: *R.M.S.* Titanic *plate on a seat in Churchill Gardens.*

never found, but the body of Eileen was recovered, identified and buried at sea on 22 April 1912.

Eileen and Neal were not the only Wiltshire people to die that night. The Goodwin family of Melksham – Fred and Augusta Goodwin with their six children, Lillian, Charles, William, Jessie, Harold and 19-month-old Sydney, were emigrating to Canada to provide a better life for their children. All perished on the *Titanic*. A body later recovered from the water was for decades to be known as "The unknown child." With advances

in DNA testing it was finally determined in 2007 that the child was in fact Sidney Goodwin. There is a memorial plaque inside St Michael and All Angels in Melksham.

The Blue Boar Inn (SU 144 301)

There are three identical plaques all on the face of Debenhams store in Blue Boar Row, Salisbury city centre. The plaques commemorate the site of the Blue Boar Inn and the Saracen's Head Inn upon which Debenhams is now situated. Within the store there is a restaurant called the Blue Boar, remembering the

Blue Boar Row in Salisbury, the site of the Blue Boar Inn. This photograph was taken in January 2014 and shows a preserved London Routemaster bus on the occasion of a bus rally day commemorating the closure of the bus station.

One of three identical plaques outside Debenhams department store in Blue Boar Row.

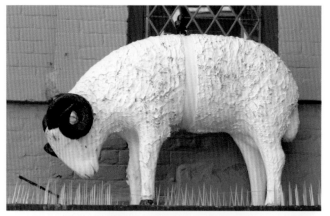

Top: *The Salisbury Ram over the shop doorway. The spikes beneath it are to keep pigeons away.*

Above: *At the south end of the High Street the original Salisbury Ram is seen above the shop doorway to the left of the gate arch.*

importance of the inn to Salisbury and the Market Square.

The Blue Boar stood on this site from the 15 century until early in the 19 century. The Saracen's Head probably replaced the Blue Boar around this time. In 1843 the site was occupied by Style and Large and later by Style and Gerrish's department store.

The plaque also records the execution of Henry, Duke of Buckingham in 1483 during the reign of Richard III.

The Salisbury Ram (SU 143 298)
On the porch roof of a shop at the south end of the High Street by the North Gate of the Close stands the Salisbury Ram. A plaque by the entrance door to the shop explains what the ram symbolises. It reads: "The wooden ram above dates from the shop's former use by Stonehenge Woollen Industries set up early in the 20 century by Catherine Lovibond, with the aim of regenerating the rural economy. The firm continued in business until 1959."

The ram was renewed in 2013 by the Salisbury Civic Society. The original ram depicted in the c.1960 photograph is different – the shape of the horns gives the game away. I do not know what happened to the original ram, which had probably deteriorated.

Miss Lovibond's father purchased Lake House in the Woodford Valley north of Salisbury in 1897. Soon after she became interested in spinning and weaving. At the time the valley lacked employment and was becoming depopulated. She had a firm desire to check this trend and set up looms and machinery on the upper floor of Lake House. Local women learned the process and were given employment and a small rural industry was established.

After initial difficulties in the sale of the cloth, the Stonehenge Woollen Industry, as it was known, exhibited at the Albert Hall in 1900. This was a success and the cloth became popular and in demand. In 1919 a spinning and weaving class had been set up for disabled servicemen from the First World War. About 1920 the concern moved to Stratford sub Castle and Amesbury, then Salisbury. There were shops in London and one in Salisbury High Street, which closed in 1959.

The Tollgate Inn Mural (SU 150 297)
The modern mural painted by Sixpenny Handley artist, Robin Budden, is situated on the once Tollgate Inn, which was closed in 2008 by Hall and Woodhouse. The building is Grade II listed and was purchased by Jim and Pam Butt at auction and was featured in the television programme *Homes Under the Hammer*. Approval

The Tollgate Mural is affixed high on the wall of the refurbished premises.

was given to convert the premises to four dwellings and this was carried out by the company, S. J. Butt and Sons Ltd. I personally visited the Tollgate during conversion and it has been very tastefully adapted to the change of use. The Tollgate Inn was previously known as the New Inn and is of seventeenth/eighteenth century origin. The Tollgate was given a Civic Society Award in 2015 for the sympathetic conversion of this listed building.

The mural itself has been personalised to feature members of the Butt family, with Jim Butt taking centre stage behind the inner pair of horses. There are many birds and animals in the picture as this is another feature of Mr Butt's business as a poultry breeder and dealer. His dog "Buttons" is standing on top of the stage coach.

Lloyds Bank Sculptured Group (SU 144 301)

On the roof of Lloyds Bank in Blue Boar Row is a sculpture of female figures on a plinth sitting either side of an armorial crest. There is a date tablet of 1869 between the figures, presumably the date this bank building was built. Unfortunately the whole sculpture is covered in anti pigeon spikes – I think I would rather have the pigeons! The building was once the Wilts and Dorset bank, established in 1835 in Salisbury and taken over by Lloyds in 1914.

Salisbury Cathedral West Front (SU 142 295)

One can argue that the whole of the west front of Salisbury Cathedral is a work of art, in so much that there are 78 statuary sculptures and one eagle in niches, from top to bottom. A number of the upper niches are empty, but would have originally contained figures.

A large number of the figures were replaced between 1867 and 1871 by James Redfern. Only six of the original statues still exist, all from the fourteenth century, Peter and Paul among them. There have been a few more recent replacements by Jason Battle.

In the picture (opposite top) there are five figures shown. From left to right: Bishop Bridport, one of the original fourteenth-century figures, Bishop Poore, Henry III, Saint Edmund of Canterbury and Bishop

The west front of Salisbury Cathedral in evening light.

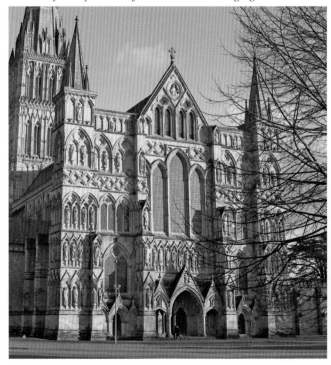

Figures on the lower left corner of the west front. Note Bishop Poore holding a model of the cathedral in his right hand.

Odo of Ramsbury. Some of the lower statuary extends around into the north face of the cathedral.

Construction of Salisbury Cathedral started in 1220 by Richard Poore after it was decided to move from Old Sarum, where the foundations of the old cathedral still exist. Richard Poore died in 1237 and the cathedral was consecrated in 1258.

Winchester Street Mosaic (SU 148 301)

The final pieces of the Winchester Street mosaic were placed in the artwork by the general public, giving the work that community touch. The mosaic is made of matt porcelain coloured tesserae of varying sizes and was produced by Joanna Dewfall and the project co-ordinated by Claire Christopher.

The process used to create the mosaic is by the "indirect" method. The tiles are stuck individually to a backing paper using dilute washable PVA glue. The completed paper faced sections of mosaic are set into flexible adhesive onto warm up board that is placed inside a metal tray. Once in position the backing paper is wetted to release the glue, then it is peeled off. The glue is cleaned off the surface of the tesserae before grouting to complete.

The mosaic reflects upon the area's past before the ring road was built in the 1970s. After completion it was placed on a wall below the ring road adjacent to a pedestrian underpass. A plaque to its side explains the content of the mural.

Joanna Dewfall's mosaic mural inside St Edmund's Art Centre in preparation on 7 March 2015. The public were invited to place pieces in the border.

The completed mosaic situated at the end of Winchester Street next to a pedestrian underpass below Salisbury's ring road.

"Go to Mould's when you're hungry" refers to a restaurant selling faggots and peas until the mid 1930s. "The Anchor when you're dry" is the Anchor and Hope pub a short distance away. "Go to Churchill's when you're tired" refers to the Churchill's rudimentary lodging house, with little more than small rooms with very basic communal toilet arrangements. "Go to heaven when you die" is self explanatory.

Other features are the traffic in Winchester Street, a steam roller, children playing, the old sweet shop and bakery, the Cyclist's Rest offering a wide range of services to the touring cyclist and locals lost on the *Titanic*, including Eileen McNamee, who is remembered on a mural in Milford Street and a seat in Churchill Gardens.

Mosaic Murals Greencroft Subway (SU 149 303)

I doubt many residents in Salisbury not living near the Greencroft are aware of the seven mosaic mural panels in the underpass between the Greencroft and Rampart Road. They brighten up an otherwise dingy subway, but such an environment, out of the gaze of the public eye, encourages less qualified artists to spray their own paint designs on the panels. When I photographed the panels in March 2015 they were relatively clean, albeit the monkey and the tree in the first panel had suffered some green daubing. I apologise to the creators for some flash reflection on some of the tesserae on the second and sixth panels.

They were created by a participatory project led by Joanna Dewfall for St Edmunds Community Association. For example, viewing from left to right row to row, the first mosaic was made by the clientele of the Winchester Gate public house, the second panel was made by members of a Mental Health Day Therapy Group and the third mosaic is clearly produced by the pupils in a local school. On the second row the first mosaic celebrates the Greencroft itself between 1365 and 2004 when the mosaic was produced. Around the perimeter are the words:

"Allow liberty to all people for walking and using lawful recreation there at all times." This refers to the Greencroft as common land. The skulls and bones could refer to the Saxon burials or plague victims buried there after the middle of the sixteenth century.

*Mosaic Murals
Greencroft
Subway.*

The jester and sheep remember the Michaelmas Fair held on the Greencroft after 1570. On a darker note, and not on the panel, executions were held there after c 1550. The fifth panel I am unsure of the participants. The sixth panel was made by Salisbury Youth Club and the final panel by the clientele of the Wyndham Arms public house.

St Thomas à Becket Doom Painting (SU 143 300)

Above the chancel arch in St Thomas à Becket church in the centre of Salisbury is the best preserved Doom painting in England. Doom or Domesday represents the final judgement. The painting depicts Christ sitting before New Jerusalem with 12 apostles at his feet. Viewing the painting, on the right of Christ is John the Baptist and left is the Virgin Mary.

On the lower left are the dead rising from their graves going to heaven and others being pulled, on the right of the painting, into the jaws of hell, represented by a dragon-like creature. It also shows the bishop being dragged into hell.

Four faces on the window lintels of a shop in Winchester Street, Salisbury.

The painting dates from 1475, but was whitewashed over in 1593. It was rediscovered in 1819, but not restored until 1881 and received further restoration in 1953. There are other smaller medieval paintings in the church as well as some worthy stained glass. The church welcomes visitors, but to show your appreciation place a donation in the church funds box please.

The Angel Gabriel (SU 143 295)

The sculpture of Angel Gabriel stands on a bronze plinth under cedar trees on the Cathedral Cloister Garden. Unfortunately its position under the trees has attracted algae and lichen. The work is by Emily Young and formed part of a temporary art installation in the early twenty-firsy century. Fortunately the sculpture in Purbeck limestone is now a permanent feature on the garden lawn.

The Angel Gabriel in the Cloister Garden of Salisbury Cathedral.

Face Masks (SU 146 301)

On the window lintels of a shop in Winchester Street are faces in relief, some are repeated. The book *Salisbury in Detail* tells us that the heads are made of Coade Stone, a type of fired ceramic material. They appear to be twentieth century as the face on the top left looks like Churchill. The identities of the remainder are unknown, although I suggest that the top right

could be Thomas Cromwell and the lower right has the appearance of Mr Hyde from Jekyll and Hyde. I am unable to make a suggestion for the happy face on the lower left, someone will no doubt enlighten me.

Clock Tower (SU 142 299)

Salisbury's tall clock tower is a landmark in the city and stands adjacent to Fisherton Bridge over the River Avon. The site was originally part of Fisherton Gaol and the large square base around the tower was part of the gaol wall. At the time the clock was built the plot lay at the corner of the Infirmary.

The clock tower has four illuminated dials and was built in in 1892-3 on the instructions of Dr John Roberts, who was honorary consulting physician at the Infirmary. He held the post until the end of his life in 1906. During this time he had built up a large private practice in the city. His wife died in 1892 and it is to she that he dedicated the clock.

A recessed arched panel reads: "This Clock Tower, built in the year 1892-3, was presented to the City by Dr Roberts who erected the same in memory of Arabella his beloved wife, the daughter of Robert Hahnam Kelham Esq. of Bleasby Hall, Notts. William Marlow Mayor 1891. Arthur Whitehead Mayor 1892. Mr Charles Powling Town Clerk."

Three possible sites were considered for the position of the clock within the city. To some the Market Square was an obvious choice, as it would have been a centre-piece in the centre of the city. I am not sure the exact position the clock would have taken up, but both the

Top: *Fisherton Street and the Clock Tower seen in c1906. Note some of the infirmary buildings have been demolished and shops have taken their place.*

Above: *The Clock Tower seen in 2012.*

centre of the square and adjacent to Blue Boar Row must have received consideration. Another site was on the corner of Catherine Street with Milford Street, but his would probably have caused congestion. The favoured location was the a corner of the Infirmary, where it is now situated.

The clock movement was supplied by John Smiths and Sons of Derby, a well respected turret clock maker, still in existence today. Originally the clock was operated by gravity-fed weights and required winding, probably once a week. In 1970 the mechanism was exchanged by Smiths for a modern system. It was further improved in 1997.

Old George Hotel (SU 143 298)

In the entrance to the Old George Mall in Salisbury High Street on a supporting vertical timber is a polished brass plate explaining the significance of this old hotel. Many visitors and residents to Salisbury pass the plate without noticing it.

The plate reads: "The Great Hall is thought to date from the reign of Edward II, but the façade is largely fifteenth century with later bay windows. The inn is first mentioned in 1378 and was bought by the City Corporation who owned it until 1863 when the licence lapsed.

Samuel Pepys stayed here in 1668 and at that time plays were acted in the yard and the Free School was held here.

The ground floor was removed and a new steel frame inserted in 1967 by the Hammerson Group of Companies as part of the Old George Mall Shopping Centre to which the new arcade now forms the main entrance.

The post on which this plaque is fixed was hand carved by a local craftsman to match the other which is original. The Granite Setts which are recessed into the paving mark the position of the original timber posts."

The plaque mentions that Samuel Pepys stayed in the inn, he is said to have enjoyed the "silke bed", but complained about the bill. Shakespeare may have entertained in the courtyard. Buddy Holly and the Crickets stayed in the hotel in 1958 while playing at the Gaumont. Less impressive, but nevertheless important to my wife was that her father, Norman, often enjoyed a pint there during his lunch break from the furniture and carpet store, Shepherd and Hedger, opposite (now Poundland).

The remainder of the building after modification to provide the Mall entrance is Grade I listed and dates from the fourteenth century and later, according to the official listing. It is now occupied by "The Boston Tea Party", which is a coffee and eating house.

The Old George 2010 and 1910.

Above: *The Cathedral Close Wall in Exeter Street.*

Below: *There are various sculpted stones from the old cathedral at Old Sarum set into the wall, many examples near the Cathedral School entrance.*

Cathedral Close Walls (SU 145 293)

The ordnance survey reference is the location of the photograph.

At the Exeter Street Gate to the Close is a tablet fixed to the wall proclaiming the origin of the stone for the Close Walls. It reads: "In the year 1331 King Edward III granted to the Bishop and the Dean and Chapter the stone of the walls of the Norman Cathedral at Old Sarum for the building of the tower of the Cathedral and the wall with battlements about the Close." Not all the wall we see today was built in the fourteenth century – some rebuilding and modifications have taken place.

There are very few remains at Old Sarum Cathedral above foundation level and any remains that exist have little or no facing stones left, even the castle facing stones must have been used. After the Cathedral tower and Close Walls had been built, if there was any worked stone left over I have no doubt a great deal of plundering for ready-made building blocks would have taken place.

At the south end of Exeter Street the masons that built it have left their inscribed marks on the wall. Most are lines both straight and curved with angles and intersections, but one I found looked like a rather plump chicken, unless it was an example of fourteenth-century graffiti!

The wall around the Close has four original gates and one nineteenth century gate built for the Bishop Wordsworth School entrance. The original gates are St Anne's Gate, Queen's Gate, High Street Gate and St Nicholas (Harnham) Gate.

Guildhall (SU 146 300)

There is a conflict of dates regarding the erection of the Guildhall. The plaque on the roof has a date of 1794 and another on the front of the building at eye level has 1795. If the plaque was made prior to completion and expecting a finish date in 1794, this may explain the year difference. The eye level plaque has more information - it reads:

"Presented to the City by the 2nd Earl of Radnor. Designed by Sir Robert Taylor, built in 1795 to replace a Tudor house damaged by fire."

The building is Grade II* listed, which states that it was designed by Sir Robert Taylor and built with alterations by William Pilkington in 1788 - 1795. Pilkington was a pupil of Taylor and took over the Guildhall project in 1788 when Taylor died. Other notable architectural works by William Pilkington were the Custom House in Portsmouth (1785) and the Naval Hospital at Great Yarmouth (1809 - 1811).

The first Guildhall in Salisbury was the medieval Bishop's Guildhall. In 1585 the Merchant's Guildhall was built near the site of the present War Memorial and this was locally known as "The Council House". This was burnt down in 1780, so the Tudor house mentioned as damaged by fire was in fact the Merchant's Guildhall. When the Bishop's Guildhall was demolished, I am uncertain. To add to the mystery of demolition there are two paintings of the old Halls by H. Hussey, which

The Guildhall taken before shoppers walk to and fro in front of the building. At roof level in the centre is a plaque, the words of which can only be easily read with magnification.

The Odeon Cinema frontage. Ye Halle of John Halle is beyond the foyer.

were painted in 1883 and 1884! Of course not possible if one was burnt down in 1780 and the new Guildhall was built in 1795 possibly on the site of the Bishop's Guildhall. Certainly the Merchant's painting was painted as it existed in the seventeenth century and one must assume the same historicism applies to the Bishop's Guildhall painting, which shows it in a state of disrepair with men on the roof, possibly being demolished.

In the present Guildhall in the twentieth century there were courts in the building and prison (holding) cells, built in 1889, in the basement. Nowadays the Guildhall is a popular venue for weddings, conferences, meetings, exhibitions and events. One of the old courtrooms, the Oak Courtroom, still remains but is not used to part people for prison terms but as a wedding venue to join them together. As I write the building is receiving a facelift.

Ye Halle of John Halle and Cinema (SU 145 299)

There is a plaque and a framed script inside the hall which is accessible beyond the cinema lobby during opening hours. The plaque reads:

"Built 1470-1483 by John Halle. Later used as an Inn. Restored by A.W. Pugin, 1834. Plaque presented by Rank Leisure Services."

John Halle died in 1479 so he did not see the building completed. He was a wool merchant, Mayor of Salisbury four times between 1451 and 1465 and M.P. four times between 1453 and 1461. He also ended up in the Tower for a time over a land dispute with the Bishop.

The reference to an inn is in 1669 when John Aubrey, the seventeenth century travelling antiquary, recorded that it was a tavern. In the nineteenth century it was occupied by the *Wiltshire Gazette* and was restored by Pugin in 1834. The north front (pictured) was added in 1881.

In 1931 the hall was incorporated into a cinema by F.E. West, architect to Gaumont British Pictures. The cinema, originally the Gaumont with a single screen and stage, was designed on a Tudor theme and is to the rear of the hall. The hall is Grade I listed and the cinema, now the Odeon, is sub-divided into five screens.

Ye Olde Corner Shop (SU 144 300)

This attractive property is on the corner of Silver Street and Minster Street. There is a wooden plaque at first floor level, which is very difficult to read even with magnification. However, it says:

"This house built in 1428 was bequeathed to the Hospital of the Holy Trinity by John Wynchestre (Barber) in AD 1447. Restored in 1912. Purchased by Joseph Powney in 1927."

John Wynchestre left his home to the Trinity Hospital (founded by Agnes Bottenham in 1379) after his wife, Agnes, died. There were conditions attached to the bequest: A mass for his and his wife's soul should be held on Friday in the first week of Lent in the church of St Thomas each year. At this time the Master of Trinity should pay to the priest and the poor in that church a decreed sum of money to be divided equally and that the Warden of the Fraternity of Barbers, to which John Wynchestre must have belonged, another decreed sum of money.

In 1875, according to Kelly's business directory, Joseph Powney had a boot and shoe business at 36 Minster Street. His shop was called Ye Old Corner Shop and according to the plaque he purchased the premises in 1927.

In 1954 it was taken over by a shoe retailing chain, and is now occupied by ShakeAway. Adjacent to the building and attached is The Haunch of Venison, seen in the right of the picture. The building is mainly fifteenth century with eighteenth century alterations. There is a macabre smoke-preserved mummified hand beyond a gated bread oven, believed to have been lost in a game of whist by a an irrational crazy player.

Castle Street Gate (SU 145 304)

Adjacent to Hussey's Almshouses on a wall in Castle Street is a relic of the Castle Street Gate forming part of the fortifications of Salisbury in 1378. The gate and west buttress were removed in 1788 and the east buttress in 1906.

A much worn relic of a Lion and Unicorn from the Castle Street Gate placed in 1908.

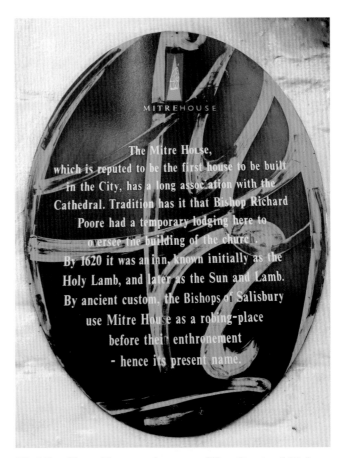

The Mitre House Plaque on the corner of New Street and High Street.

Mitre House (SU 143 298)

The plaque is positioned on what is believed to be the site of the first house in Salisbury. Tradition has it that Bishop Poore had a lodging in Mitre House where he could oversee the building of the Cathedral, commenced in 1220. Mitre House is so called because it is used as a dressing house before enthronement of new Bishops of Salisbury.

Poultry Cross (SU 144 300)

The Poultry Cross stands at the junction of Silver Street and Minster Street. It is Grade I listed and is an hexagonal open-arched shelter with a central column. The whole of the roof has been rebuilt with a central roof column supported with flying buttresses between 1852 and 1854 to a design by Owen Brown Carter.

Turner painted the Poultry Cross from a Butcher Row viewpoint in c. 1800. The roof appeared relatively flat with a low central column rising to a square four-faced sundial. Probably only three of the faces had a gnomon to cast a shadow. Surrounding the cross on the north and west sides were low capped walls – not part of the structure. The Grade I listing calls them seats, but Turner's painting shows them unsuitable to sit on.

There is a bronze plaque inside the cross on the central pillar, which reads:

"This structure, known as the Poultry Cross as early as 1335, is one of four market crosses which formerly

Harnham Bridge, Salisbury (SU 144 291)

There are two adjacent bridges spanning the Avon, separating the City of Salisbury from Harnham. Between the bridges, which I will call lesser and greater, is an island. In the photograph showing the road towards St Nicholas Hospital over the lesser of the two bridges, the houses in the foreground are built on the island. The commemoration stone is situated on the left parapet of the bridge

The plaque records that the bridge was built by Bishop Bingham in 1243 and was widened in 1774. There is a Grade I listing for this bridge, which gives a building date of 1244. Perhaps building commenced in 1243 and was completed in 1244. The greater of the two bridges has six arches and the lesser two. The old original bridge is encased with improvements made in the sixteenth - seventeenth centuries and of course by bridge widening in 1774.

The listing refers to the bridge as being described with two names: Ayleswade or Old Harnham. I found the name "Ayleswade" puzzling., so with reference to a book entitled *Wiltshire Place Names* (see bibliography) the following came to light. In 1255 the bridge built by Bishop Bingham was called Pontem de Ayleswad, a combination of Latin and Saxon words. I was already aware that pontem is Latin for bridge and wad/waed were Saxon words for wade or ford. Ayles has been interpreted as Aegel's. So we have Bridge of Aegel's ford. This shows that the river was forded here before the bridge was built.

stood in Salisbury. The others were the Cheese Cross, the Linen Cross and Bernewell Cross. The low wall which enclosed this cross was removed in 1853."

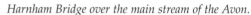
Harnham Bridge over the main stream of the Avon.

The Pheasant Inn.

Above: *The lesser of the two Harnham bridges in which is set the stone. The view is along St Nicholas Road towards St Nicholas Hospital (almshouses).*

Left: *The Bishop Bingham commemoration stone set into the parapet of Harnham Bridge.*

Robert de Bingham was ordained in 1229 succeeding Bishop Poore. Adjacent to the lesser bridge on the east bank of the river and south of the road is St Nicholas Hospital. Bishop Bingham is credited with founding the hospital and certainly made very substantial improvements to existing buildings, which probably existed since 1215, the date of original founding recorded on a gate plaque. It is probable that the hospital improved facilities and the bridges were constructed at a similar time. On the central island the hospital has a chapel connected by a footbridge.

Bishop Bingham died in 1246, only two years after he saw his bridge works completed.

The Pheasant Inn (SU 146 302)

The Pheasant Inn is Grade II* listed and was built in the fifteenth century. It is two storey timber framed with brick and plaster filling. Crewe's Hall is on the first floor and is accessed via stairs in the courtyard. A plaque reads: "Originally The Crispin Inn. This building incorporates the Shoemakers Guildhall left to the guild in 1638 by Philip Crewe in memory of his father." The Crispin Inn was named after the patron saint of Shoemakers.

Crewe's Hall was part of a complex of buildings left to the Guild of Shoemakers by Philip Crewe, the son of a shoemaker in 1638. The building became the Crispin Inn in c. 1743 with a covenant on the Hall for the Guild's use. In c. 1821 the building was leased and it became the Pheasant Inn. It was sold in 1828 and the covenant was dropped.

Salisbury – Queen's Arms (SU 146 298)

The Queen's Arms in Ivy Street lays claim to holding the longest continuous licence in Salisbury, since 1558. Until recently (2015) the commemoration plaque on the side of the public house was a red oval matching the other signage on the building. It has changed to a large circular blue plaque, but has the same wording, presumably to match the Salisbury Civic Society blue plaque scheme in the city.

The plaque reads: "Queens Arms - 1558 - Salisbury. Licenced in 1558, the year Queen Elizabeth I was proclaimed Queen of England. This house can claim to have the longest held continuous licence in the City of Salisbury. Prior to becoming an inn it had been bequeathed to the Dean and Chapter of the Cathedral in 1400."

The present building dates from the early eighteenth century, but altered in the nineteenth century according to the Grade II listing. Clearly the Queen's Arms as a named public house on this site has held the licence, not the actual building, which must have been rebuilt.

Right: *A long standing oval red plaque has only recently been replaced with this blue one – the words are the same.*

Below: *The frontage of the Queen's Arms is in Ivy Street. There is a very attractive arched shell roof on the porch.*

Salisbury – Miscellaneous Commemorations

As already mentioned the number of commemorative plaques in Salisbury is prolific. Here I conclude the Salisbury commemorations with the remainder that are worthy of mention.

Of the days of stage coaches there are two reminders of this mode of travel. Outside the Red Lion in Milford Street is a plaque commemorating a daily stage coach service from the hotel, which was previously called the Red lion and Cross Keys (SU 147 299). There is no mention of the destination of the stage. The plaque also mentions that part of the site was used in 1280-1320 as a hostel for draughtsmen working on the construction of the Cathedral. In Brown Street a plaque on the site of the eighteenth century Black Horse Inn (SU 146 301) recalls the fast stage leaving for London twice a week.

The library at the junction of Castle Street and Blue Boar Row is embellished with a number of commemorations (SU 144 301). The top of the building has a clock made by Blick National. It is an electric clock of no particular interest except a plaque next to the library passage states that it was presented to the City by Salisbury Rotary Club in commemoration of the Silver Jubilee of Queen Elizabeth II. Blick were well known for manufacturing time recorders for factories, known as "clocking in and off clocks" Another plaque commemorates the start of construction of the library in 1973 and another commemorates its opening in 1975. Not withstanding these three plaques there is another commemorating the site of the Cheese Cross where milk and cheese were sold in pre-reformation days. The plaque also states that the Franciscan Friars possibly preached at this spot.

The mention of Franciscan Friars takes us to another plaque at (SU 147 304) in The Friary, recording that in c. 1225 Franciscan Friars established a religious house near this place. The monastery was dissolved in 1538 during the reign of Henry VIII and his arguments with Rome over his wish to divorce Catherine of Aragon, which resulted in the birth of the Church of England. Another plaque relating to the Friars is in St Anne Street (SU 147 296) which commemorates the acquisition of the property by William Windover, merchant, in the sixteenth century. It carries on to say that Richard II and Queen Ann feasted the Franciscan Friars Minor here in 1393.

On the corner of Barnard Street and Culver Street (SU 148 297) a plaque commemorates the site of the Cattle Market and cross known as Barnwell's Cross. There seem to be alternative ways of spelling the cross name. On the Poultry Cross plaque it is spelt Bernewell's Cross. Apparently the market spread into the neighbouring streets during busy times of the year. In the present Market Square adjacent to the War Memorial is a paving slab marked the site of the Time Capsule (SU 145 300). There is no indication on the slab when it was placed there, what it contains or what year in the future it is scheduled to be opened.

We find out what was opened in 1748 in Salt Lane (SU 146 302) "with a goodly feast and much strong beer" – The Weavers' Guild. It only commemorates the site of their Guildhall. In Chipper Lane on the side of a building is a large panel with lettering in relief. It commemorates the Edwin Young Gallery built in 1913, which contained at the time 500 or so watercolours painted by Edwin Young of Salisbury and its environs. The library now has an Edwin Young Gallery with some of his pictures displayed together with other artists – entry is free.

There are restored almshouses in Fisherton Street, with a plaque set into a wall at pavement level commemorating Mrs Sarah Haytor, Lady of the Manor, 1797 (SU 139 301). Sarah Haytor originally endowed the almshouses.

There is a very elaborate plaque beside the gateway to Council House in Bourne Hill (SU 147 304). It commemorates the College of St Edmund from 1268 to 1546, which stood in these grounds. The present large house standing on this site, which now has the offices of the registrar, was built in the eighteenth century.

Finally a bridge over the River Avon on Scamell's Road (SU 142 307) has two almost identical cast iron plaques on each side of the ironwork. I say "almost" because the word "formerly" is spelt "formely" on one side. The bridge once carried the L.S.W.R. over Castle Street until it was removed and placed in its present position by T. Scamell in 1898. Emphasis is made of the fact that no machinery was used in its repositioning. I suppose the company moving it had a team of strong men all called "Atlas"! The bridge was made by Joseph Butler and Co., Stanningly Iron Works, near Leeds in 1857.

Spotlight on Saxon Crosses

There is a number of Saxon cross shafts in churches in Wiltshire, but no circle and cross symbols remain to surmount any of the shafts. The crosses are often referred to as Celtic crosses and have symbolic figuring, interwoven and geometric designs. During the pre Norman Conquest era some of the crosses would have been religious icons in significant locations for Saxon Britain. The Normans seemed to have no regard for these religious symbols and used them as wall infill when they rebuilt or erected their own churches.

Parts of Saxon crosses have been found in walling when churches have been rebuilt. How many more have these historic remains hidden inside medieval church structures?

Codford St Peters (ST 966 399) is one such example. A pristine Saxon shaft was discovered buried within a wall when the church was substantially altered in the mid 1860s. The cross shaft is believed to date from c. 800 AD. The condition of the shaft and lack of weathering suggest it has never stood outside in the open air.

The shaft shows a man holding foliage in one hand and an axe-like tool in the other. It appears he has chopped off the branch of foliage from a tree or bush and is holding it in the air. Above the foliage at the top of the shaft are some geometric designs. The symbolism of the carvings is difficult to interpret.

Another almost complete Saxon shaft, but reassembled, is inside Ramsbury Holy Cross church (SU 274 716). Once again during restoration of the church, this time in 1891, a number of Saxon artefacts were removed from the south wall, including parts from two Celtic crosses with intricate designs and ornate coffin lids. They were used as infill in the wall of the present church which was started in the thirteenth century.

The three large fragments

The Saxon cross shaft in the chancel of St Peter's church in Codford.

Left: *A reassembled Saxon cross shaft in Ramsbury Holy Cross church, with an ornate coffin lid from the Saxon period in the foreground.*

Below: *Fragments of a Saxon cross and a Norman carved figure in Colerne church.*

put back together date from the ninth - eleventh centuries. Locals refer to it as the "Great Cross of Ramsbury." It has interlacing work over a serpent. The interlacing seems to be a continuation of the serpent's tail. It is also seen biting its own body. There is also knotwork and circles in the design.

In St John the Baptist church in Colerne (ST 821 712) there are three architectural fragments built into a wall. The two outer stones are parts of a Saxon cross said to have been erected at Colerne to commemorate St Aldhelm, Bishop of Sherborne who died in 709AD. The cross itself is later. Aldhelm's body rested at Colerne on its way for burial in Malmesbury Abbey.

The central figure is not Saxon, but dates from c. 1200AD and is possibly part of a wall Panel.

St Sampson's church in Cricklade (SU 099 935) has a Saxon cross shaft built into the wall over the north door. It is dated to the tenth century and has interlaced carving.

St Laurence's church in Bradford on Avon is an original Saxon church with no out of period alterations or rebuilding, beyond repair work. I include it here for its uniqueness and it has a Saxon cross within, albeit a

fragment and the remainder simulated. It was possibly founded by St Aldhelm c. 700AD, although the architectural style suggests a later date in the Saxon period. So it is all of Saxon origin, but possibly adapted or rebuilt during this period.

Previously the church had been a school, a house and even a warehouse before, in 1856, its significance was realised. It seems to reach for the sky, has a north porticus (large entrance porch) and at one time had a similar feature facing south. The evidence is left in the shape of the roof in the masonry. The main body of the church has a chancel, seen on the right of the photograph, wherein there is a stone altar and the Saxon cross above it.

Right: The fragment and simulation of the Saxon cross in St Laurence's church in Bradford on Avon. The stone for the simulation was found around the church.

Far right: The larger part of a Saxon cross inside the porch and in the wall over the north door of St Sampson's in Cricklade.

Below: A rare example of a church from the Saxon period – St Laurence's in Bradford on Avon.

Savernake

Mystery Monument (SU 231 662)

While walking in Savernake Forest near Grand Avenue I came across a very dilapidated monument surrounded by protective metal railings. It appeared to have had a gated access, but the gate was missing. On one of the faces of the rectangular block body is an empty recess. This must have contained a memorial bronze plate describing the circumstances behind the placing of such a monument in the middle of Savernake forest.

I can find no confirmed information about this relic, but I suspect it to be for a person who died in the forest, possibly at this spot. The railings suggest a private memorial for a person of some standing, possibly from the 19th century.

There is hearsay regarding a female rider meeting her death in a fall from a horse in circumstances that are unknown.

More macabre are tales of a ghostly headless woman rider emerging from the autumn mist at dusk on a large white charger galloping at speed along the Grand Avenue.   Perhaps more have seen such a ghostly apparition than are prepared to admit. Others have heard the rustling of autumn beech leaves and the movement of brushwood, then the sound of a bolting horse and a chill breeze as it rushes by - not the time to remain in the forest when darkness descends!

Apparently the ghostly rider relates to unsubstantiated tales of a Royal hunting party with one of the group being a lady rider on a large white horse. A sudden sound, possibly the firing of a gun, spooked the horse and it bolted through the wood with the rider hanging on for grim death. The trees were huddled together and the branches low, one of which struck the rider fair and square on the forehead and decapitated her.

Are the monument and the tales connected? - maybe wishful thinking! - Who knows? - Someone does.

George III Column (SU 229 648)

This 90 ft. column was erected by Thomas Bruce, Earl of Ailesbury, in 1781 as a memorial to George III. It is sited as a viewpoint from Tottenham House at that time the Earl's residence. It is Grade II listed and has a square base with inscriptions, an unfluted column rising to an Ionic capital with a drum above it and topped with a bronze urn.

There are two commemorative plaques set into two recesses of the column base. One commemorates the erection of the column as a testimony of gratitude to the Earl's uncle Charles Earl of Ailesbury and Elgin, who left him the estate.   It also confirms the Earl of Ailesbury's loyalty to George III who conferred on Thomas Bruce the honour of the Earldom. The tablet is dated 1781.

A second tablet dated 1789 commemorates the restoration of perfect health to George III from a long and afflicting disorder.   In fact the inscription was premature as we all are familiar with "The Madness of King George". For a long time after he died in 1820 he was believed to have suffered from an hereditary physical disease called porphyria , for which one of the signs are blue urine. However more modern thinking considers he had a psychiatric illness. It is known he took gentian as a medication for his troubles, which also turns urine blue.

The column was originally erected in a field to the east of Brandenburgh House near Hammersmith as a memorial to George Doddington, Lord Melcombe, who died in 1762. He was an English politician and nobleman. I do not know whether it was given to or purchased by the Earl of Ailesbury. It seems odd that a monument should be rededicated to someone else, albeit George III.

Bruce Tunnel, Kennett and Avon Canal (SU 236 632)

Bruce Tunnel on the Kennet and Avon Canal is 502 yards long. The tunnel bore has a cross section larger than average. In fact it is the second largest, after a canal tunnel in Birmingham, of any on a British canal. In the days of horse towing, chains were provided low near the water the whole length of the tunnel so that the barge could be man hauled along. The chains can still be seen from the entrance on the right hand wall of the tunnel going east to west. There is no towpath through the tunnel, which meant horses had to be taken over the rise in land to the other end of the tunnel to wait for the barge. Once the barge had momentum I suppose pulling on the chains wasn't as arduous as one might imagine. Certainly not so strenuous on some of the small bore tunnels where the bargee had to lie on the roof and leg it through on the roof of the canal.

Top: *The eastern entrance to Bruce Tunnel.*

Above: *The replacement plaque on Bruce Tunnel. The original above the tunnel entrance has become illegible.*

The tunnel is named Bruce after Thomas Brudenell-Bruce, 1st Earl of Ailesbury (now spelt Aylesbury), through whose land the canal needed passage. The tunnel was begun in 1806 and was finished in 1809 and opened in 1810. It was a requirement of canal passage set out by Thomas Bruce that a tunnel was bored under the rising contours on his land. Actually a deep cutting would also have sufficed and it would have been less expensive, although when the Great Western Railway was built the canal would have been an obstacle to pass over.

Over the eastern entrance portal is a large slab of stone with inscriptions, which have become impossible to read as the limestone is delaminating and flaking off, but I suppose it has been there for over 200 years. Fortunately a smaller copy of the words has been placed at eye level on the brick wall of the tunnel entrance. It reads:

"The Kennet and Avon Canal Company inscribe this tunnel with the name BRUCE in testimony of the gratitude for the uniform and effectual support of the Right Honourable Thomas Bruce, Earl of Ailesbury and Charles Lord Bruce his son. Through the whole progress of this great national work by which a direct communication by water was opened between the cities of London and Bristol. Anno Domini 1810."

Underneath this large inscribed slab is a smaller slate plaque describing the circumstances of the replacement dedication. It reads:

"This monument was erected by the Kennet and Avon Canal Partnership and John Lloyd, seventh generation mason of Bedwyn as a replica of that erected by his ancestor, Benjamin Lloyd, mason of Bedwyn to the Kennet and Avon Canal Company. Anno Domini 2003."

Seend

Horse Pond (ST 948 612)

At the eastern end of the village at Threeways is a pond which has been fenced, but has some history to impart. A plaque on an angled stone plinth records the story:

"It is believed that this historic village feature has existed in this location since the 18th century, providing

a watering place for cattle and other livestock. The separate cobbled area was provided for horses to water during journeys between local towns. The pond was restored in 1996 by Lynwell Ltd. Under the direction of Kennet District Council."

Seend Cleeve

Iron Works (ST 932 614 site of plaque)

It is feasible that iron ore has been mined and smelted on here a small scale since the Iron Age, but it wasn't until c. 1850 that the ore was mined on a commercial basis. A tramway with wagons pulled by horses was built from the mine to the Kennet and Avon Canal at Seend Cleeve, near the present location of the Barge Inn. The Kennet and Avon Canal was opened in 1810 and barging minerals was the most economical transportation method of the time. Fortunately Seend was below the Caen Hill flight of locks. From Seend the ore was shipped along the canal to Bristol, where it was transferred to a small sea-going sailing ships to cross the channel to the smelters in South Wales.

The ore was of high quality with few impurities, but it did not suit the Welsh smelters and payment for the ore was low, perhaps by design to protect their own supply or for technical reasons. There were other options in the Midlands, but there were transportation difficulties. Thus it was in the interests of the owners, who by 1857, were the great Western Ore Company, to smelt their own ore into pig iron. Smelters were built, which at the height of production could produce 300 tons of iron in total per week. Although there were three 50 ft. high blast furnaces, only two of them seem to have been used. In addition to the smelters there were four hot air ovens, a beam engine and some gas apparatus.

Pig iron is the intermediate product of smelting iron ore with a high carbon fuel such as coke or anthracite using limestone as a flux. Coke was produced in South Wales and anthracite was mined in West Glamorgan. Both could be brought in by rail. Wiltshire had pride in smelting its own ore and a large lump of pig iron was exhibited in Devizes Market Place.

A broad gauge railway line was built by the Great Western Railway from Holt Junction to Devizes in 1857, which resulted in a connection to the Iron Works. It was at this time that the railway must have taken over the transportation of the pig iron and also brought high carbon fuel in to fire the furnaces. In 1862 the line was extended from Devizes to the Berks and Hants line at Patney and Chirton. However, incoming and outgoing traffic to and from the mine would have, in the main, been via Holt Junction.

Unfortunately the company were unsuccessful, it is believed through mismanagement, and bankruptcy proceedings were started. The Wiltshire Iron Company took over the business, but this also failed. Smelting ceased at the site in c. 1876. In 1889 the Iron Works were demolished, but ore continued to be mined until 1946.

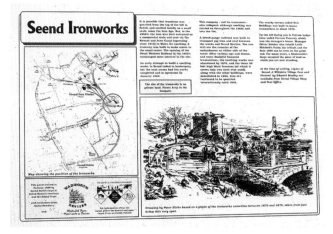

From top: *The Iron Works plaque by Seend Cleeve canal bridge. Seend Iron Works from a photograph held in the Wiltshire Museum archives; probably taken in c. 1880, prior to its demolition in 1889. The site of the Iron Works seen from the canal lock at Seend Cleeve below the bridge. Mining for the iron ore was conducted beyond the works. The railway track bed connecting the Works with Seend goods yard seen from above the canal at the bridge.*

Sevenhampton

Ian Fleming (SU 209 903)

Ian Lancaster Fleming (1908 - 1964) was an English author, journalist and naval intelligence officer He is famous for his series of novels about 007, James Bond. He used his wartime intelligence experience as a foundation for his spy books. Most of his books have been made into films. Indeed his first book, *Casino Royale*, published in 1953, has been filmed twice in 1967 and 2006. His own personal favourite, *From Russia with Love*, was published in 1957 and made into a film in 1963. The first of his books to reach the cinema was *Dr No* in 1962. I remember seeing this and thought it a new style of explosive entertainment. He also wrote *Chitty Chitty Bang Bang*, of course, also made into a much loved film.

He lived in Sevenhampton during his latter years and is buried in the churchyard with his wife Ann and their son Casper, who took his own life at the age of twenty-three.

The grave of James Bond-author Ian Fleming.

Shalbourne

Jethro Tull (SU 316 635)

There is a memorial tablet inside St Michael's church in Shalbourne to the memory of Jethro Tull, the famous agriculturalist. Jethro Tull was born in 1674 and baptised in Lower Basildon Church in Berkshire and was buried there in 1740. Later in life he lived and worked at Prosperous Farm in Shalbourne, which at the time of his death was actually in Berkshire. Boundary changes in the late nineteenth century placed Shalbourne within Wiltshire.

The commemoration to Jethro Tull in St Michael's church in Shalbourne.

The tablet places him in history as a pioneer of British agriculture and quotes from his book *Horse-Hoeing Husbandry*:

"Tis in some degree the interest of every one who lives by bread that true principles be established in agriculture: but none ought to be allowed as such, till they have been thoroughly examined. Truth is like gold which the more it is tried the brighter it appears, being freed from dross."

The tablet is blacked bronze and has not taken well to flash photography. It was placed there by the Agricultural Education Association in 1932.

He invented, among other implements, the horse drawn seed drill, which economically spread seed in neat rows, and the horse drawn hoe. He also advocated that by tilling the soil well the same crop can be planted year after a year – probably his only faux-pas.

The 1967 rock band from Luton was named Jethro Tull after him.

Shaw

Christchurch Tower (ST 888 657)

The tower of Christchurch in Shaw is richly decorated with statues and flying gargoyles. Among the statues depicted on the tower corners are David, Daniel, Isaiah and Zephaniah. Over the west window is the Good Shepherd and lower down by the doorway are Gabriel and the Madonna.

The first church on the site was small and built in

1838. As the congregation grew with the expansion of the village, a much larger church was required. Thus, in 1905, it was rebuilt to a design of C.E. Ponting in a late perpendicular style.

Two niches on the corner of the tower of Christchurch, Shaw, show Isaiah and Zephaniah with a projecting gargoyle separating them.

Sherston

Rattlebone Statue (ST 853 860)

The Church of the Holy Cross in Sherston has an origin dating back to Saxon times in the ninth century. However, only fragments remain from this period. A Norman church followed in the late twelfth century and there are remains of this. Over the centuries many additions and alterations have taken place. A major restoration took place in 1876-7.

On the exterior of the church in the junction of the eastern wall of the porch with the nave is a sculpted figure once thought to be the Saxon warrior John Rattlebone. The statue is holding something over his chest, for a long time believed to be a tile covering a wound.

John Rattlebone, a local Saxon leader, was believed to be part of the Saxon army that in 1016 fought Cnut the Great near Sherston. John Rattlebone was mortally wounded in the battle and is said to have staunched his wound with a stone tile from a local quarry. Hence the belief that the sculpture held a tile to his chest.

Unfortunately the statue is of a priest holding a book – a case of wishful thinking to glorify local history.

Why was he called Rattlebone? Saxon armour was simple and cheap to create – a bag of bones around the neck would have prevented a fatal blow and severing of the head – Maybe?

John Rattlebone or a priest?

Albert Titanic Chadwick (ST 853 860)

In the churchyard of the Holy Cross in Sherston is a gravestone dedicated to Albert Titanic Chadwick. His middle name suggests he was born on the *Titanic* the day the ship struck an iceberg on 14 April 1912. Albert survived until April 19th 1983. The commemoration stone also has the following words: "Calm after the storm, sinking of the Titanic."

I am unable to find any person with the surname Chadwick on the boarding list. Neither have I established that any baby was born on the *Titanic*. However, there were a number of expectant mothers on board. There was a great sense of loss among the population upon the sinking of the ship and the huge drowning toll. It was not uncommon at the time to name babies born on 12 April 1912 with a middle name "Titanic" as a mark of commemoration of the disaster.

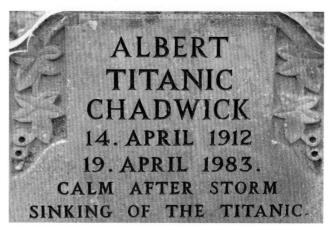

Shrewton

Cecil Chubb and Stonehenge (SU 069 443)

In the High Street in Shrewton there is a plaque on the side of a house, easy to see travelling up the street from the south, commemorating the birthplace of Sir Cecil Chubb (1876 - 1934) who gave Stonehenge to the nation on 26 October, 1918.

Three years earlier he had purchased the most famous set of stones, probably in the world, with 30 acres of surrounding land at auction for £6600. The auction took place in the Palace Theatre in Salisbury on 21 September, 1915. He had attended the auction out of

interest, but when lot 15 came up he thought "a Salisbury man ought to buy it", so he placed a bid and won. I wonder what was said when he went home and told his wife "I've just bought some stones."

On 26 October 1918 he handed over Stonehenge and the land to Sir Alfred Mond, First Commissioner of Works. There were two conditions attached to the gift by Cecil Chubb. The first was that all the gate takings for the rest of the war were to be given to the Red Cross. Of course this was for only a short period of time as the war ended on 11 November 1918. The second condition was relevant to all the residents of Shrewton and the parishes in the Amesbury Rural District; they were to get free admission during normal opening hours. I wonder if anyone has told the National Trust and English Heritage!

Flood Cottages (SU 069 435)

I use the Shrewton Flood Cottages as an example, but the same event in 1841 affected Maddington, Orcheston, Tilshead and Winterbourne Stoke, where there are also Flood Cottages. That isn't to say the floods were restricted to the Till Valley, where all these villages are situated, but wider afield on the Salisbury Plain and its surrounding habitation.

After new year in 1841 the weather turned extremely cold with temperatures down to well below freezing for an extended period of time causing an almost perma-frost situation. To add to this extreme cold it snowed heavily causing deep snow and drifting everywhere.

On 16 January the wind changed direction and very mild air swept in causing a rapid thaw. The ground was still frozen underneath the snow and the rapid melt caused vast lagoons of water to build up on the plain. As the thaw progressed the lakes of water were released into the normally quiet and often dry water courses. Torrents of water rushed into the villages causing flash floods. The swirling maelstrom under-

mined the cheaply made cob cottages and caused many of them to collapse and wash away. Some writing on the event say it was raining heavily adding to the volume of water.

In Shrewton alone three lives were lost, 130 people were rendered homeless and 28 cottages destroyed. There was mud and ruin everywhere. This was a disaster on a massive scale the like of which had never been experienced before. Committees were set up quickly to raise funds by public subscription to alleviate the misery of the homeless. By 1842, 14 cottages had been built in the Till Valley villages affected. The cottages were built of brick and rendered then painted white (at least that is how they appear today). Any relief fund money left over after the cottage buildings were finished and an

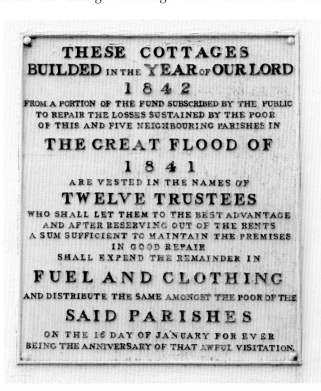

THESE COTTAGES BUILDED IN THE YEAR OF OUR LORD 1842 FROM A PORTION OF THE FUND SUBSCRIBED BY THE PUBLIC TO REPAIR THE LOSSES SUSTAINED BY THE POOR OF THIS AND FIVE NEIGHBOURING PARISHES IN THE GREAT FLOOD OF 1841 ARE VESTED IN THE NAMES OF TWELVE TRUSTEES WHO SHALL LET THEM TO THE BEST ADVANTAGE AND AFTER RESERVING OUT OF THE RENTS A SUM SUFFICIENT TO MAINTAIN THE PREMISES IN GOOD REPAIR SHALL EXPEND THE REMAINDER IN FUEL AND CLOTHING AND DISTRIBUTE THE SAME AMONGST THE POOR OF THE SAID PARISHES ON THE 16 DAY OF JANUARY FOR EVER BEING THE ANNIVERSARY OF THAT AWFUL VISITATION.

allowance made for maintenance, was allocated for fuel and clothing for the poor of the parishes.

On each of the cottage blocks there is a plaque commemorating the building of the cottages. The plaque records that the cottages are vested in the names of 12 trustees. I believe the cottages are now let to the elderly of the villages that apply to the trustees, who vet the applicants for suitability. I suppose in such circumstances they are classified as almshouses.

Snap

Lost Medieval Hamlet (SU 223 764)

There are many medieval village hamlet sites in Wiltshire, Snap is but one of them. However, there is one major difference with Snap to the others – its final demise occurred in the early years of the twentieth century.

Being classified as a medieval village or hamlet does not necessarily imply that its origins were in medieval times – some habitations may have begun in Romano/British or the Saxon period.

However, the first record for Snap was in 1268 when it was called Snape and later listed as Snappe, but there is archaeological evidence to suggest Snap is much older than the thirteenth century. There is very little to see today, all that remains is hidden in a copse, a few scattered pieces of stone building material. The green lane that runs south of the site was at one time the village's main street, although it is difficult to imagine that a rutted stony track was once the hamlet's High Street, although probably not named as such.

The population of Snap, numbering never more than 50, existed with the working members of each household being employed on the local farms, which were engaged in arable practices. Everything began to change when the vast prairies of America were farmed for grain. Imports into Great Britain of cheaper corn in the 1870s caused a depression in the arable farming industry, such that it became uneconomical to compete. Farms converted to pasture and farmed sheep and cattle. The need for Snap farm workers quickly reduced, causing the families to move away to seek employment elsewhere. By 1905 only one elderly lady was in occupation in the hamlet, and when she passed on the village became derelict. During this depressing period the land was purchased by Henry Wilson, who grazed sheep for his butchery business. Building materials were salvaged from the site and used elsewhere, but there were still remnants of the farmhouse in the 1930s.

Among other medieval sites in Wiltshire, which may have earthworks to see, I name the following: Bupton (ST 058 761), Chilhampton (SU 093 333), Henset (SU 240 682), Shaw (SU 136 652), Upham, north of Snap (SU 225 774) and Woodhill (ST 060 770). Woodhill is interesting in so much that it had a windmill, which had become redundant by the seventeenth century. There is a mill mound recorded on the ordnance survey map at ST 055 767. This would proba-

bly have originally been a post mill with its cross tree support buried in the mound. The reasons for each village's demise are varied, but converting land to pasture for sheep must have played its part.

Snap can only be reached on foot. The memorial tablet is small and was almost hidden from view by a small fallen tree when I visited the site in the spring of 2015. The footpath across the meadow is not recommended, as a patch between two stiles on the end other side of the meadow is tangled with brambles – I had the scratches to prove it!

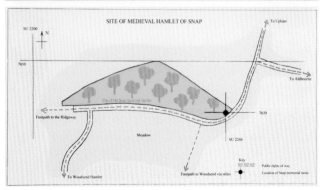

From top: *The memorial to the people of Snap.*
Nothing remains of Snap, a copse covers the site of the hamlet.
Site map of Snap hamlet. (not to scale).

South Marston

Concorde Model (SU 181 888)

Very much a piece of art is this model of a Concorde displayed on a post at the junction of Stirling Road and Spitfire Way, South Marston Business Park. The area was once a wartime aircraft factory and airfield. The model is, unfortunately, not in pristine condition and could do with a clean and polish.

The Concorde project was a joint venture between Aerospatiale (France) and BAC Concorde. It was a turbojet-powered supersonic airliner that reached 1350 mph and could travel between London and New York in a little less than 3.5 hours. The engines were Rolls Royce/Snecma Olympus 593, which gave the aeroplane a range of 4143 miles on full tanks carrying 100 passengers.

The first two built were prototypes, one was built in France and the other in England. The aeroplane's first flight was on 2 March 1969. The first commercial flight was between London, Heathrow and Bahrain, which took place in 1976. I remember the proud moments when I regularly saw it after take off when I lived near Reading. If my memory serves me correctly it was after just after 11 am, the distinctive ripping sound of the accelerating engines as the delta winged wonder went on its way.

Not all ran smoothly for the Concorde for there was a serious accident on 25 July 2000, when a Paris to New York flight crashed shortly after take-off killing all 100 passengers and 9 crew on board. One of the tyres suffered a blow out on the runway, which in turn caused the fuel tank to rupture and the aircraft caught fire. Concorde was retired from service in 2003.

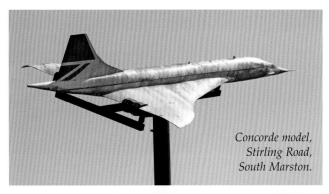

Concorde model, Stirling Road, South Marston.

The real thing, reg. G-BOAG, taking off with wheels retracting.

A model of a Spitfire in Spitfire Way, South Marston.

A Spitfire in flight seen from the ramparts of Old Sarum.

Spitfire Model (SU 181 890)

The Spitfire is the most iconic aeroplane of the Second World War. It always sends a shiver down my spine when I see one and hear the distinctive Rolls Royce Merlin engine. The model, now with rather faded camouflage, is situated on a post in Spitfire Way in South Marston Business Park.

It was a single seater fighter plane used by the RAF and other Allied countries during and after the Second World War. Its elliptical wing gave it an unmistakeable appearance during flight and could reach 360 mph. Its manoeuvrability and speed made it more than a match for the German Me109.

It was designed by R.J. Mitchell and was a descendent of the floatplane designed by Mitchell to compete in the flying race for the Schneider Trophy. The first prototype flew in 1936 and production took place between 1938 and 1948. Over 20,000 were built and it continued in RAF front line service until 1954. The Seafire was a variant of the Supermarine Spitfire.

I doubt that there are any modern air shows without a flypast of a Spitfire, Hurricane and Lancaster bomber.

Alfred Williams (SU 194 879)
and Jubilee Stone   (SU 195 879)

Alfred Williams (1877 - 1930) was born and died in South Marston. He was an author and poet, little known outside his local environment. In addition to the commemorations in South Marston village he is commemorated alongside Richard Jefferies on a standing stone near Barbury Castle.

He was born in Cambria Cottage and there is a plaque to commemorate the fact. The plaque calls him

The plaques on Cambria Cottage and on Rose Cottage in South Marston where Alfred Williams was born and lived, respectively.

The War Memorial and Jubilee Stone with Rose Cottage in the left background. And a close up of the Jubilee Stone.

a "Hammerman Poet". I assume this refers to him as working in the forge and stamping shop at Swindon Railway Works. If there is another explanation I would be pleased to hear it. He was employed in the Great Western Railway Works for twenty-three years and this took a toll on his health.

There is another plaque situated on Rose Cottage only a short distance from Cambria Cottage and he lived there between 1881 and 1903. He married Mary Perk in 1903 and moved into Dryden Cottage, again only a stone's throw from where he was born.

His heart was really in the countryside and he began to express himself in poetry and published *Songs in Wiltshire* in 1909, followed by *Poems in Wiltshire* in 1911. Arguably his best work was *Life in a Railway Factory*, which he dared not publish until he left the railway's employment in 1914. He then joined the army and became a gunner in the Royal Field Artillery and served in India. Upon his return to England his spell in India had rekindled his enthusiasm for writing.

By 1930 his health had deteriorated, furthermore his wife had been diagnosed with terminal cancer. He died in April 1930 and his wife died a few weeks later.

Within sight of Alfred William's Home at Rose Cottage is a Jubilee Stone placed on a small green next to the War Memorial, which commemorates the Golden Jubilee of Queen Elizabeth II in 2002.

Stert

James Long Monument (SU 030 598)

James Long of Urchfont in 1768 promoted a new road from Nursteed in Devizes to Lydeway in Urchfont. The existing road, which was turnpike in 1707 was steep and arduous. Of course the traffic in those days wasn't engine powered, but horsepower. Hills must have been difficult for horses pulling heavily-laden carts to negotiate and reach the summit.

The monument is situated inside the fork of a road to Etchilhampton from the main A342 between Devizes and Upavon. The road constructed in 1768 remains in use today as part of the A342. The monument itself is Grade II listed and is made of limestone. The lion, at the time of grading for listing purposes to effect protection for the future, had a paw missing and was noted with a metal tail. The difference in materials for the tail is obvious in the photograph. I suspect that at some time in the distant past the lion was damaged and the tail replaced. There is a plaque on the body of the monument which reads:

"An: Dom: 1771. This monument, from a general sense of gratitude, was erected to the memory of James Long, late of Wedhampton, Esqr., whose publick spirit of benevolence which he ever exercised for the service of mankind were remarkably exerted in planning, promoting and completing this new road. An: Dom: 1768, by which a former tedious and dangerous way over the adjacent hill is avoided, to the great pleasure

James Long monument.

Stockton mosaic memorial.

Stockton

Mosaic Memorial (ST 982 382)

This mosaic memorial is inside the church of St John the Baptist in Stockton in the Wylye Valley. It is situated to the side and rear of the font and is a memorial to Arthur John Barrington Yeatman, youngest son of Huyshe, Lord Bishop of Southwark and Lady Barbara Yeatman.

Arthur was born on 11 October 1882 and died before his twelfth birthday on 9 September 1893.

There is a booklet available in the church regarding the church history and artefacts. It states that the baptistery mosaic was carried out by Italian workmen in 1879. This obviously refers to the floor, since the son of the bishop died in 1893. I imagine that the wall mosaic in whole or in part must have been placed in or after that year.

Mosaic Floor (ST 982 382)

The baptistery floor mosaic in St John the Baptist was undertaken by Italian workmen. Compare this with that of the Downton Roman villa mosaic on display in Salisbury Museum in Cathedral Close. It is noticeable that the tesserae colour palette is very similar, albeit that the Roman tiles dating from between 300 and 400A.D. have suffered the ravages of time and have

and convenience of travellers."

There are a few words in Latin which I have omitted. I have punctuated the dedication, but not amended the spelling. It is also noted that the dedication has every low case letter "s" written in old English as if it was an "f". For the unsuspecting this makes it very difficult to read!

The mosaic floors in Stockton church (above) and Salisbury Museum (opposite, bottom). One nineteenth century Italian and the other from the Roman period in Britain.

become muted.

The Downton Villa mosaic was unearthed in Moot Close, Downton, in the 1950s. It was believed to be the floor of a possible dining room of a long narrow building with seven rooms. There are no visible surface remains on the site of the villa. With regard to the Stockton baptistery floor, I have been unable to establish why an Italian mosaic should have been commissioned for Stockton church, but it was installed during the church restoration of 1879.

Stourton

Obelisk (ST 773 345)

The obelisk is situated at the end of Fir Walk above the gardens at Stourhead. It is Grade I listed and has a sun disc with a face and sun's rays emanating from it at the top of the column. The base is made of green limestone and the column has a tapered shaft made of Bath stone.

The obelisk was erected in 1746, but the original decayed and became dangerous and was replaced in 1839. Further damage was sustained in 1853 when it was struck by lightning. I suspect the smiling metal sun at the top of the column had something to do with it! There is a memorial tablet in Latin to Henry Hoare added in 1815 by Richard Colt Hoare.

Henry Hoare I purchased Stourton House in 1717 and smartly demolished it and built in its place a Palladian mansion, which he renamed Stourhead, so named because the source of the River Stour was on his land. The source is now marked with St Peter's Pump. The obelisk was built by Henry Hoare II in 1746 as an example of the antique obelisks of Rome. He was also responsible for creating the gardens, so popular with the visiting public.

The Stourton obelisk topped by a radiant sun. Lightning has struck the tower in the past and there is now a lightning conductor to earth any future strike.

King Alfred's Tower – adopted!
(ST 746 351)

King Alfred's Tower is 161 feet high (49 metres) and is actually a folly, serving no useful purpose other than providing a viewpoint over the Stourhead estate, Wiltshire and Somerset. Although built as part of the estate it is actually in Somerset in Brewham parish, although at the time of building it was said to straddle three counties, Wilts, Somerset and Dorset. The Dorset border is south of this spot and it would take a great deal of boundary investigations over the past centuries to determine whether there is any factual support for this, but it could explain why it has a triangular shape with towers in each corner.

The tower was conceived by Henry Hoare II in 1762 and designed by Henry Flitcroft in 1765. It was completed in 1772. There is a spiral staircase in one corner which takes the paying public to the top of the tower after climbing 205 steps. The photograph shows the glorious viewpoint, which takes in a full 360 degrees. Henry Hoare dedicated the tower to the accession to the throne of George III and the end of the Seven Years War with France.

The tower was damaged by a plane in 1944 and was restored in the 1980s. The repaired brickwork in the tower shows as a lighter patch. Since then the tower has deteriorated, but funding has been made available to restore the tower's stonework near the top.

Swallowcliffe

Site of St Peter's Church (ST 966 271)

The original church of St Peter's in Swallowcliffe was built in the twelfth century on the east side of a tributary of the River Nadder. The commemoration stone gives an earlier date of c. 940 AD indicating the belief that a church stood on this site about 200 years earlier.

The church consisted of a nave, transept and partial south and north aisles. A tower was added in the fifteenth century. When the surrounding land was further developed in the eighteenth and early nineteenth centuries, the church became prone to flooding. In bad winters the stream welled up with rushing water from Swallowcliffe Down to the south, which rises steeply to 221 metres. Floodwater entered the church and the level in the nave could be severe enough to cover the seating, leaving a muddy residue when the water subsided. Flooding became such a problem that the building was declared unsafe and unusable in 1840. The church was abandoned and plans laid to build a new St Peter's.

The old St Peter's was demolished in 1843 and a new church built a short distance away on higher

ground using much of the original stone in its construction. A fourteenth-century stone knight, believed to be Sir Thomas West, was moved into the porch of the new church.

To include King Alfred's Tower in Wiltshire may be considered cheating, as it is yards inside the Somerset border and in a different parish. However, it is considered part of the Stourhead estate visiting package. In any case the shadow cast by the tower in the late afternoon probably falls into Wiltshire, so I lay claim to include it.

The fact that King Alfred rallied his troops nearby at the site of Egbert's Stone in 878 before the Battle of Edington (Ethandun) gave Henry Hoare a third reason of dedication. Indeed he made the most of it with a commemorative tablet and a statue of Alfred in a niche over the door. The tablet reads:

"Alfred the Great, A.D. 879, on this summit erected his standard against Danish invaders. To him we owe the origin of juries, the establishment of a militia, the creation of a naval force. Alfred the light of a benighted age was a philosopher and a Christian. The father of his people. The founder of the English Monarchy and liberty." There is a memorial stone on Bratton Down near the Westbury White Horse commemorating the site of the battle. Note that the tablet has an incorrect date of 879 instead of 878.

The commemoration to the old church of St Peter's in Swallowcliffe that was abandoned in 1843 due to regular flood problems in winter.

Swanborough

Swanborough Tump - Commemoration Stone
(SU 130 601)

The Commemoration Stone at Swanborough Tump has three commemorative plaques affixed. Two relate to the Swanborough Hundred and the other to the meeting of Alfred with his older brother in 871 A.D. The later will be explored in a future volume concerning military matters.

The stone was originally set up to commemorate the Swanborough Hundred moot (meeting) place. The plaque reads:

"Swanborough Tump. Swinebeorg. C. 850. The meeting place of the Hundred of Swanborough."

The actual Swanborough Tump I believe to be the remains of a bronze age round barrow. It was the meeting place in Saxon times where elders of the Hundred would meet to make decisions. The Hundred referred to land which could sustain 100 households, each household/family would have an elder to speak for them.

A later derivation of a Hundred would be a geographical division to divide a region into smaller administrative divisions. So the Swanborough Hundred by the early nineteenth century had Great

Cheveril (detached) in the west, All Cannings to the north, Market Lavington and Upavon in the south and the Manningfords in the east and of course all the villages within the Hundred boundary. By the end of the nineteenth century the Hundreds were replaced by urban and rural districts.

The more recent plaque fixed above the stone relates to a gathering of families who bear the Swanborough name. The plaque reads:

"29th July 2000. A gathering was held at this site of families who bear the Swanborough name and whose origins can be traced to this Hundred."

Swindon

Villett's House (SU 157 838)

According to John Betjemen this is "the finest house in Swindon"? The house is facing Cricklade Street and was built in 1729 by the Harding family. It was sold in 1770 to the Villette family, hence the name of the house. The façade of the house is of Flemish brick with ashlar limestone dressings. The window lintels have grotesque faces in low relief. The property is Grade II* listed.

In 2007 when workers where converting the property to luxury flats during drainage operations a network of tunnels were found. Where all the tunnels lead to is a matter of speculation since the various routes are blocked up. It is apparently well known in the town that Old Town had a network of tunnels connecting various properties and even extended out to Coate Water. Quite why the

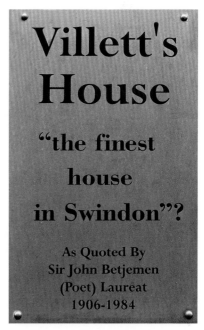

Villett's House plaque, Swindon.

tunnels where routed to or via Villett's House is not known, but there is speculation that smuggling activities and the movement of alcohol may have some connection. One usually associates smuggling with the coast and access to the sea, but I suppose the Wilts and Berks Canal had access to the coast eventually, but any contraband would have taken weeks to reach Swindon.

The John Betjemen quotation is, I believe, in *Studies in the History of Swindon* published in 1950.

Swanborough Tump Commemorations.

Station Jubilee Clock (SU 150 852)

The Golden Jubilee Clock situated in the station forecourt at Swindon railway station was originally installed in Canal Walk in the town centre in 2002. The

clock's time keeping was an issue and it was removed from its position in 2009 to be replaced by a water feature. The clock was stored for a time, but it had been intended to place it in its present position, fittingly in time for the Queen's Diamond Jubilee.

The clock is illuminated at night – I hope it keeps time in this location as it is far more important for passengers catching trains than it is ambling through the shopping centre!

G.J. Churchward Grave (SU 158 849)

George Jackson Churchward was born in Stoke Gabriel in 1857. He started his railway career as an apprentice in Newton Abbot, Devon, railway workshops. He moved to Swindon Works to work under Joseph Armstrong, Chief Mechanical Engineer of the Great Western Railway between 1864 to 1877. In 1900, while working at Swindon Works he became Mayor of the new Swindon, when old and new became one town.

He rose through the ranks at Swindon and became chief assistant to Armstrong's successor, William Dean. Dean was Chief Mechanical Engineer between 1877 and 1902. In 1902 Churchward took over as C.M.E. for the Great Western Railway. During Dean's last years he and Churchward collaborated on a new design of 4-4-0 tender engine termed the *City* class. Included in this batch of locomotives was the famous *City of Truro* famed for its high speed run with the *Ocean Mails* on 9 May 1904, It was during this run that the locomotive was credited at the time with 102.4 m.p.h

His locomotive designs were appealing-looking machines, some might say elegant. In 1902 the *Saints* were introduced and in 1906 the *Stars*, both of a 4-6-0 wheel arrangement which he preferred for the metal road to the West Country with its sharp curves and steep banks.

Among Churchward's other designs were the 2800 heavy freight engines 4700 class, nicknamed "Night Owls" as they were often used at night and the 4500 class tank engines.

Churchward retired in 1921. On one misty morning

From top: *The grave of Churchward in Christ Church, Old Swindon. Churchward's design of heavy freight locomotive 28XX class no. 3834 passing Iver, Bucks, with a freight on 10 April 1960; it had recently been overhauled in Swindon Works. A scene inside "A" shop, Swindon Works, where Churchward built his engines.*

in December 1933 he was walking along the track to visit the works from his house close to the railway and was struck by an express and died. He is buried in Christ Church graveyard in Old Swindon.

The importance of the Railway Works and the Great Western Railway to Swindon was immense and is the reason for the very existence of the New Town and Brunel's railway village. Churchward is part of this heritage.

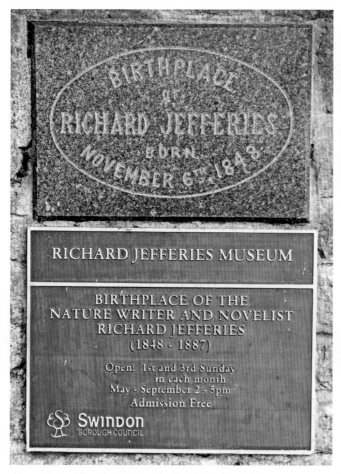

Above left: *The plaques outside the Richard Jefferies Museum Farmhouse, where he was born in 1848.*
Top right: *Coate Farmhouse, now the Richard Jefferies Museum.*
Above right: *The Council Oak by Coate Water mentioned in one of his books (ST 178 825).*

Richard Jefferies – Coate Farmhouse (ST 179 829)

Richard Jefferies was born at Coate Farmhouse in 1848 and wrote books and essays on farming and rural life together with novels, some about childhood, reflecting upon his own experiences. The farmhouse and surroundings formed the background to many of his novels.

Standing at the edge of Coate Water, near the farmhouse is the Council Oak, which featured in a book called *Bevis, the Story of a Boy*. There is a plaque beneath the tree recording the fact. Unfortunately the tree is in poor condition, with a large part of the upper trunk lying near by.

Other books include *The Story of my Heart*, 1883; *Round About a Great Estate*, 1880; *After London*, (science fiction), 1885; *Toilers in the Field*, published after his death in 1895.

Richard Jefferies suffered from TB and other ailments for much of his adult life. Illness did not prevent him from putting pen to paper and his writings are quite numerous. He died in Worthing on 14 August 1887.

In the grounds of the farmhouse is a plaque under a young apple tree; it dedicates the tree to the memory of Mark Daniel who saved the Richard Jefferies Russet apple. There are many forms of Russet apple depending upon the degree of russeting (roughish olive/brown skin) and taste. The orchard at the farm had a special cultivar, which died in 1999. The tree had been propagated with twig cuttings with some difficulty, but now the variety is grown at a number of locations in the south and west.

Mentioned earlier in the Gazetteer is a memorial near Barbury Castle to Jefferies and Alfred Williams, both Wiltshire naturalists and writers.

The Wish Hounds (SU 154 820)

The Wish Hounds are situated in a clearing in Croft Wood, Swindon. They are best appreciated at dusk as long as you are not afraid of the dark! They bound across the sky in search of prey. In full daylight they are seen supported on long stilts and have far less menace. They were created in 1993 by Lou Hamilton with scrap steel welded together.

The hounds are based upon folklore and West Country legend and are frequently associated with Dartmoor in Devon. They are said to be the hounds of hell, supernatural dogs in British mythology with glowing red eyes. However, the hounds are not confined to the west, they are said to stalk lonely places in the south of England. Beware the black cloaked huntsman and his pack of snarling dogs, teeth glistening in the moonlight, emerging from the mist just after the sun goes down – the red-eyed hounds of hell!

There are other names given to the Wish Hounds: Yell, Yeth and Marsh dogs. It is probable that Sir Arthur Conan Doyle was aware of these legends when he wrote *The Hound of the Baskervilles*.

The sinister Wish Hounds in Croft Wood, Swindon.

The Blondinis balance on a ball recollecting one of their acrobatic feats.

The Blondinis (SU 151 856)

The sculpture of the Blondinis is situated in St Marks Recreation Ground. They were an acrobatic circus troupe of the 1920s performing in circuses in Swindon and elsewhere. The 17 foot high statue was sculpted by John Clinch and was cast in aluminium in Swindon Railway Works shortly before it closed in 1986. The Railway Works foundry was situated opposite the building now housing the Great Western Steam Museum. I visited the works many times in the 1960s on conducted Sunday tours and remember the casting boxes filled with compacted sand.

The brightly coloured statue was originally erected in the Wharf Green area of Swindon, but was removed in 2005 when the area was regenerated. In 2009 it was restored and unveiled again in the St Marks Recreation Ground in Gorse Hill, Swindon. It now overlooks a revamped children's play area – one hopes the children do not attempt the acrobatic feats of the Blondinis!

Diana Dors Statue (SU 118 847)

Diana Dors is situated outside Cineworld in a leisure complex at Shaw Ridge, Swindon. She was commissioned by Thamesdown Borough Council and unveiled in 1991. Diana is the work of John Clinch and is cast in bronze.

A study of Diana Dors in a film premiere photographic pose as a blond bombshell.

"Film Star" 1931 ★ 1984

Diana was born Diana Mary Fluck in Swindon. Her film career started in 1947 and her many films included *Oliver Twist* in 1948, *A Kid for Two Farthings* in 1955, *Yield to the Night* in 1956 and she played a Madam in Western *Hannie Caulder* in 1971. She also made many television appearances on programmes like *Blankety Blank* and *Celebrity Squares*. As a chat show guest she was also very popular.

I. K. Brunel Statue (SU 148 847)

The statue of Isambard Kingdom Brunel (1806-1859) was unveiled by Sir James Jones KCB, Permanent Secretary for the Department of the Environment, to commemorate the inauguration of the first stage of the Brunel Centre on 29 March 1973. I am told that the statue is capable of playing classical music through grilles in it's plinth.

Isambard was born in Portsmouth in 1806 and following in his father's footsteps, becoming a mechanical and civil engineer involved with the first tunnel under the Thames in London. In 1833 he was appointed Chief Engineer of the fledgling Great Western Railway. By1838 his chosen broad gauge had reached the Thames. He bridged it with the "Sounding Arch", which everyone thought would collapse due to the shallow-arched design. Needless to say it still carries the railway over the Thames at Maidenhead today. When the railway reached Swindon he built the Railway Works (now closed), which is the main reason Swindon has expanded into a major town.

He is justly famous for his steamship SS *Great Britain*, which is restored in dry dock in Bristol Harbour, Paddington and Bristol Temple Meads stations, Clifton Suspension Bridge and Box Tunnel. His final masterpiece is the Royal Albert Bridge spanning the Tamar at Saltash. Unfortunately its magnificence is marred by the adjacent road bridge.

Isambard Kingdom Brunel stands in Swindon town centre, by the shopping mall named after him.

The Jubilee or Golden Lion (SU 149 847)

The Jubilee Lion sits on a plinth in The Parade in Swindon town centre. The plinth records that it was placed to commemorate the Silver Jubilee of Elizabeth

Above: *Brunel statue.*
Below: *The Golden Lion greets shoppers in The Parade, Swindon.*

II 1952 - 1977. It was unveiled in 1978. The plinth was, upon installation, made of brick, but c. 2010 the plinth was replaced with tapered marble. It certainly looks better in marble, but suffers from lime seepage at the joints.

The sculpture is not the original Golden Lion that graced the public house by the same name, once sited here by the Wilts and Berks Canal. The original lion was situated over the entrance to the pub, but it became insecure and was removed into the garden near the canal.

The Wilts and Berks Canal Trust website sheds more light on the fate of the original lion. The public house closed in 1956 and the lion was stored under wraps to protect it. Unfortunately the covers had the opposite effect to protection – condensation caused the stone to deteriorate and crumble. The Golden Lion was no more!

Stacked Fountain   (SU 149 847)

Stacked Fountain is situated in the town centre in a pedestrian crossways near The Parade. It was commissioned by Swindon Forward and is owned by Swindon Borough Council. It was designed by Walter Jack Studio and made by Richard Stump and John Hall. The sculpture cost nearly a quarter of a million pounds and was installed in 2010.

It is designed to have running water flushed over its curvature. There are approximately 1000 slices of stainless steel, cut by Premier Laser, in the sculpture.

Water Feature   (SU 127 847)

The sculpture is in the Quadrant Delta Business Park, Swindon. It is titled "Water Feature" by Nick Moore and was installed in 1990 (opposite page, above).

Although it was originally a water feature of three figures holding up a bowl of water with a circular reservoir at the artwork's base, the reservoir has been filled with soil and planted. The reason for this is unclear, but it still sits impressively in its surroundings.

The Watchers ((SU 125 838)

"The Watchers" stands on a brick plinth on the edge of the Toothill village car park. It is not in its original location having been moved a short distance to make way for a reclamation area. The sculpture represents guardian figures watching over the local community. It is made of cement fondue, which has become chipped in a few places.

The statue was sculpted by Carleton Attwood and was unveiled on 8 June 1982. A plaque cast in the casting shop at B.R.E.L. at Swindon Railway Works is situated on the front of the plinth. Another plaque on the plinth tells us that "The Watchers" statue was given as a gift to the people of Toothill by R.S. McColl and E.H. Bradley Ltd.

Above: *One of three figures holding up a water bowl, looking rather glum, in "Water Feature".*
Below: *In the modern village centre car park at Toothill in Swindon the cloaked watchers overlook the community, shrouding them against harm.*

North Star   (SU 150 848)

In a pedestrian underpass leading to the town centre are four early broad gauge locomotives as murals on tiles. The four are *Leo*, *North Star*, *Firefly* and *Vulcan*. *North Star* is depicted here.

The locomotive was built in 1837 by Robert Stephenson and Company and it had the distinction of hauling the first GWR directors special on 31st May 1838. It was improved by rebuilding with a new boiler and other refinements in 1854.

North Star was withdrawn in 1871 and scheduled for preservation. The last broad gauge lines were converted to standard gauge in 1892. For some reason the engine was broken up in 1906, but it is thought some of the locomotive parts were saved and stored.

The scrapping of *North Star* was regretted and in 1925 a replica was built in Swindon Works and placed on display at the end of the main erecting shop ("A" shop), Some of the parts from the original locomotive were used in the reconstruction. I visited the works on many occasions with my camera and remember it well. *North Star* is now on display in Swindon "Steam" museum.

Ceramic tiled representation of North Star *and broad guage replica of the engine raised on display in 1957 at the end of the erecting shop in Swindon Railway Works.*

The Arkell's Brewery mural in a prominent location at the end of a Swindon row of terraced houses.

The Golden Lion Bridge mural was based upon a turn of the century photograph. A recreation of the reflections in the water is particularly attractive.

Arkell's Brewery Mural (SU 157 855)

The mural for Arkell's Brewery is painted on the end of a terraced house in County Road, Swindon. It was originally painted by Ken White, who is a Swindon mural and canvas artist.

His most famous work was for Richard Branson's Virgin Atlantic Company – the "Scarlet Lady" logo, which appears on all Richard Branson's aircraft. His first mural was that of the Golden Lion Bridge over the Wilts and Berks Canal, shown following in this Gazetteer.

Unfortunately Ken White's most famous Swindon mural on a wall in Prospect Place, which showed celebrity Swindonians, had to be removed because the wall had damp problems affecting the property upon which it was painted.

With regard to Arkell's Brewery – John Arkell established his brewing business in Swindon Road, Stratton St Margaret, in 1843. He saw a niche market in supplying numerous local public houses with beer instead of them having to make their own. His business expanded rapidly and in 1861 he built a new steam brewery behind his own Kingsdown Inn and this followed over the years with regular additions to his bank of properties. Today Arkell's is a well known brand in and around Swindon and Wiltshire.

Golden Lion Canal Bridge Mural (SU 153 849)

Ken White painted his first mural in 1976 on the end terrace wall of a property in Medgbury Road. It showed the Golden Lion Bridge, so called because it was situated near the Golden Lion public house.

The bridge spanned the Wilts and Berks Canal at the junction of Regent Street and Bridge Street and the Golden Lion was adjacent to the towpath. I wonder how many inebriated Swindonians came out of the pub at closing time and teetered into the canal?

The Golden Lion Bridge was built in Swindon Railway Works in 1870, replacing a wooden swing bridge. There are examples of wooden swing bridges still being used on the Kennet and Avon Canal. A footbridge was added in 1877 after public subscriptions raised the finance.

The Wilts and Berks closed in 1914, the railways and steam lorries having taken its traffic. Four years later the bridges were demolished. The Golden Lion pub is remembered in The Parade in the town centre with a lion sculpture.

Applause (SU 156 837)

Clap your hands together and one can see that the hands are not clasped together, but caught in mid clap. The sculpture is made of bronze veneer, which I believe is a cold spray process, coating a substrate with thin

Above left: *"Applause" is situated outside Swindon Arts Centre.*
Above right: *The welded steel "Gorilla" is seated in Queens Park.*

The Old Wiltshire Horn.

metal and curing quickly to give the impression the sculpture is made of solid bronze. This has two obvious benefits: low weight and cost.

The sculpture is situated outside the Old Town Arts Centre and Public Library. The sculpture is called "Applause" and is by Mark Amiss. It was commissioned through Percent for Art by Swindon Borough Council in 2003.

Gorilla (SU 157 843)

Made of welded steel "Gorilla" is a sculpture by Tom Gleeson. There is another of Tom's sculptures, a metal cow, at the Great Western Hospital in Swindon. The hand has been replaced at some point as it shows a different patina to the remainder of the animal.

A plaque adds the following comments: " Unveiled by the Worshipful the Mayor of Thamesdown. Cllr. Doreen Dart. It was purchased through Percent for Art by Thamesdown Borough Council in 1985." The plaque also states that the "Gorilla" was re-sited in 1994. It is known that the "Gorilla" was purchased following an exhibition in the Theatre Square in 1985.

A comment about Queens Park. It is now a 12 acre beauty spot in the middle of Swindon, between New and Old Towns, but was once a brick works and clay pit!

The Old Wiltshire Horn (SU 159 835)

At the entrance to Dewell Mews in Swindon Old Town is this sculpture by Jon Buck of "The Old Wiltshire Horn". This local sheep was once one of the most important breeds in the country. Known for its substantial carcass, not for its wool, which is fine and minimal.

The sculpture was commissioned by Trencherwood New Homes (Western) Ltd in collaboration with Thamesdown Borough Council to commemorate the redevelopment of the old cattle market site.

Children's Mural (SU 156 844)

This mural is in Queen's Park and overlooks the lake. Drawings produced by local children were recreated in Tim Carroll's mural painted in 2007. This photograph was taken in 2015 showing the artwork has stood the test of time. Featured on the mural are flora and fauna

found in the park, including the park's metal artwork situated close by.

I imagine the children were taken to the park with their art equipment and asked to record their interpretations of the gardens and wild life on their art pads. A selection would have been made from their drawings to recreate the mural. Note one of the children has his version of the park's "Gorilla" sculpture painted on the lower left of the panel, but I am not sure any of them would have seen the fairy to the top right of centre!

In contrast to the mural's bright interpretation of the park, there is a solemn corner for reflection for all the workers in Swindon Railway Works that became ill and died from exposure to asbestos used in the insulation of locomotive boilers. It was known locally as "Swindon disease", it affected the lungs, causing breathing problems. The plot is called the Mesothelioma Garden.

Turtle Storm (SU 157 843)

This sculpture is by Joseph Ingleby, who was born in Beverley in East Yorkshire in 1962. It is called "Turtle Storm" and is situated beside a rectangular ornamental pond in Queen's Park. Interpretation for me is difficult, but I think the scallops of metal represent a throng of turtles, if these are the right words to use. It is made from welded steel, which has inevitably turned rusty giving it a patina that harmonises with the terracotta rings around the work.

To the rear of the sculpture is a water feature fountain (purposely out of focus as it wasn't the centre of attention). Each time I have visited the garden it never seems to be working. This is a very attractive part of Queen's Park gardens in the warmer months, particularly when autumn colours are reflected in the water.

Another public sculpture by Joseph Ingleby called "Flywheel" is situated in All Hallows School in Aldershot, Hampshire.

Metal Cow (SU 189 824)

This life size metal cow sculpture is in the grounds of the Great Western Hospital in Swindon. It is easily seen from the site entrance.

The Great Western Hospital opened in 2001. Previous to the sculpture's present location it was sited at the Princess Margaret Hospital in Okus Road, Swindon, which has since been demolished.

The artist is Tom Gleeson and the cow is made of welded steel. It was originally unveiled in 1987.

College Street and Edgeware Road, Homage to Tramways (SU 151 848 & SU 152 847)

There are two reminders of the tramways that once ran through the centre of Swindon in the form of stainless steel vertical artworks. One arches and the other twists, presumably simulating the pantograph pole and twisting nature of the track. Each is situated adjacent to cycle racks in roads just yards from Regent Street, the main thoroughfare where trams rumbled between Old Town, the GWR railway station, Cricklade Road and Rodbourne Road.

The first idea for a tramway for the Old and New Towns of Swindon was mooted in 1883. This was to be a steam tramway, but plans were not approved until 1899. Steam trams were abandoned in favour of electric power in tandem with the spread of the electricity network in Britain. About this time Old and New Swindon Boroughs were combined into a new Swindon Corporation.

The system was completed and opened in 1904, with the first tram running on 22 September. The track was 3ft 6 inch gauge, doubled in places so that trams could pass each other. All the routes met at the junction of Fleet with Bridge Streets and this was known as the Tram Centre, where trams could be boarded for all destinations.

There was a serious accident on 1 June 1906 caused

This has met with a lot of criticism since it was installed in 1991 as the general public have no idea what it represents. Research tells me the Chi title comes from the letter "X" in Greek, which leaves me puzzled, except that it just may represent the sound of "X" in modern Greek. Another derivation is Chinese for energy force - some people use it for their inner energy.

It was purchased by Allied Dunbar Plc and originally when it was installed it was surrounded by seating, the sculpture being the focal point. The inspiration behind the placing of the sculpture in this position is obscure, or am I missing something?

Cavendish Square Mosaics (SU 174/5 839)

The original Cavendish Square was a 1960s concrete shopping centre, which had many facilities associated with a reasonable size town. It seems that much of this has been demolished and the area regenerated, although a number of shops still remain. I believe both of the mosaics – showing a sailing ship and Cavendish Square inscription with a fish design and the avian design – were both in the shopping centre. However, the site was partially demolished in 2008 and refurbished in 2011, which is the probable reason the avian mosaic is now situated in the lawn in front of St John the Baptist's church in Whitbourne Avenue opposite the Cavendish Square shops. Placing this mosaic in the grass has done it no favours as grass is now encroaching over the design.

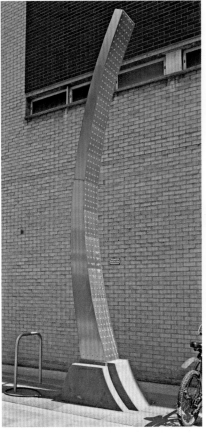

Top: *The Tram Centre, Bridge Street, 1905.*
Above left: *Homage to tramways in Swindon: artwork in College Street off Regent Street, now a pedestrian shopping precinct in New Town, but where trams ran in the early twentieth century to Old Town.*
Above right: *A similar homage to tramways in Edgeware Road off Regent Street. This one twists rather than arches.*

by brake failure on Victoria Hill. Five people died and thirty were injured. The trams' heyday in Swindon was between 1910 and 1920, after which road traffic increased. By 1928 double deck buses were ordered sounding the death knell for the tram system. The last tram ran on 11 July 1929.

Chi Sculpture (SU 151 849)

The Chi sculpture is situated near the pedestrian underpass to New Town centre below Fleming Way. It is made of steel and has weathered to a smooth rusty finish.

Sad, Happy and Indifferent (SU 173 837)

This sculpture made of corten steel, a weathering steel that takes on a light rust appearance over a number of years, is situated in a children's play area adjacent and south of Cavendish Square in Park South, Swindon The sculpture title reflects the expression on the faces of the children.

The sculpture was made by Gordon Dickenson and installed as part of a regeneration project for the area. The subject was based upon ideas presented by Park South Youth and the children of Oak Tree School.

Drum and Mural (SU153 845)

Both the drum and mural artworks are adjacent to an art workshop near Regent Circus in New Town. The drum (actually an air vent) has artwork reminiscent of ancient Central American culture painted upon it. The mural is close by on the outside wall of an art workshop. Both were blank canvases waiting to be decorated.

Both works were commissioned by Artsite, effectively commissioned by the people for the people, Both artists wish to be anonymous.

Peter Pan Statue (SU 152 834)

A statue of Peter Pan has been in Old Town Gardens in Swindon since the early 1900s. The original artist is unknown, but there are suggestions that apprentices in the railway works were responsible for its creation. I doubt this as it is almost certainly the work of one sculptor. However, there is every possibility that the figure was cast in the foundry at Swindon Works by apprentices lending some credence to the story.

The present statue is a replica of the original lead statue, which is stored in safe keeping. In 2004 the original, situated on a stone cairn near the rose garden, was beheaded by vandals. The pieces were collected and arrangements made for a foundry to put the pieces together and recast the figure. At the same time replica resin castings were made. The figure has been restored to its original position standing on its stone cairn.

Peter, looking very much like a girl, is looking skyward with his hands on his hips, hornpipe in his right hand and a rabbit at his feet.

Shop Frontage Tiling (SU 157 838)

In Wood Street in Swindon Old Town is a shop, currently "Brunettes", which has a ceramic tile panel on each side of the frontage. The photographs show a central section of each panel. In the centre are two classical heads with birds and baskets of flowers. The flower baskets are identical, but the tiles with birds depicted are all different. They show a house sparrow, starling, kingfisher, and bullfinch.

No doubt the manufacturer is British as the birds are all to be seen in Britain. They probably date from c. 1880 and may have been manufactured by a Minton company as the corner design in the tiles of the birds is typical of some of their geometric edge patterns.

Wood Street was redeveloped after the middle of the nineteenth century and 24 Wood Street was occupied by Robert Few, poulterer. He was known to be in occu-

The drum and wall mural are closely associated near Regent Circus in New Town. They are possibly artwork connected with a nearby art workshop.

pation in 1881 and was again recorded in 1889, but by 1911 he had retired. In the early twentieth century the shop was a ladies and gents tailors.

Hey Diddle Diddle (SU 109 851)

Hey Diddle Diddle is a sculpture based on the children's rhyme. It was sculpted by Vega Bermejo from Portland stone and placed on a small cultivated triangle in Spencer Close, The Prinnells, in 1992.

It was commissioned by Thamesdown Borough Council and sponsored by Clarke Holmes Ltd under the Per Cent for Art Scheme.

The lyrical sculpture has all the characters and objects featured within the rhyme, with the cat and fiddle dominating on one end and the cow on the other. The sides have all the remaining elements.

The rhyme is very familiar and some of the words date back to the sixteenth century, but words akin to the modern version date from the middle of the eighteenth century.

As I remember it from a child:
Hey diddle diddle,
The cat and the fiddle,
The cow jumped over the moon,
The little dog laughed,
To see such fun,
And the dish ran away with the spoon.

Above:
Peter Pan statue.

Left:
Shop front tiling.

Right:
Hey Diddle Diddle.

How the Mighty Fall (SU 116 848)

This cast aluminium and cast iron sculpture is by Tim Sandys-Renton and was placed in a large green public space above Shaw Ridge leisure and hotel complex. Access is easy from the adjacent car park by walking on a path up through the copse at the rear into the green open space.

The sculpture seems to represent an archaeological find from the far distant future reflecting upon our modern industrial age. The wheels have impressions of large footprints, the front side of the aluminium has two hands and arms clasped around an orifice as if shouting about misfortune.

Move to the rear of the sculpture and the orifice is now a mouth of an impressed person trapped in time.

This is a very clever and intriguing sculpture. I leave the onlooker to draw his or her conclusion on interpretation.

Looking into the Future (SU 120 843)

Looking into the Future is a three figure glass fibre structure that is now suffering the effects of vandalism and the elements. It is situated near the West Swindon Centre to the rear of a large pond, which itself requires maintenance.

The sculpture was created by Jon Buck in 1985 and shows three figures in bathing costumes in a lounging mode.

Jon Buck was the first artist in residence for West Swindon when it was being developed in the 1980s. He created the sculpture for the Westlea Play Park, but it was later relocated to its present position.

Nexus (SU 111 835)

Hideo Furuta's Nexus (binding together) sculpture is situated in Freshbrook Centre in West Swindon. It is sculpted from blue pennant stone from Pembrokeshire,

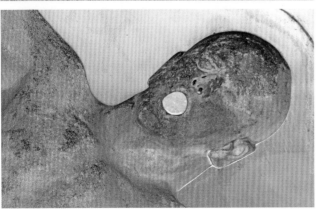

Top: *From a distance the sculpture looks like a crashed aeroplane.*
Above: *On the rear of the central feature is the impression of a body. An optical illusion makes it appear to stand out in high relief.*

From top: *Looking into the Future; Nexus; White Horse Pacified.*

the source of the blue stones at Stonehenge.

Hideo laboured for six months during 1986, in public and in situ, with hand-made tools to fashion four large stone blocks into his interlocking artwork.

The work is laid on lengths of heavy duty timber. The sculpture's main feature of two interlocking stones surmounted by a pyramid forms a bridge across the two supported pieces of art work. Some of the wooden supports have recently been replaced.

White Horse Pacified (SU 119 857)

Julie Livsey's White Horse Pacified sculpture stands in parkland adjacent to Cartwright Drive in West Swindon. It is made of steel and concrete and is an interpretation of the white chalk horses of Wiltshire. The suggestion of a rider on the horse has pacified it compared to the wild appearance of its chalk relatives.

The sculpture was completed in 1987 during an international artist exchange between Swindon and Lisbon in Portugal. It was funded by Calouste Gulbenkian Foundation, Southern Arts, Wiltshire County Council and Thamesdown Borough Council.

Once it was clearly visible from the highway, now it is backed by tall trees that have grown unhindered since it was placed

Bandstand (SU 153 834)

This very attractive bandstand in Old Town Gardens has a commemorative plaque stating it was refurbished by Swindon Borough Council, Hemmings and public donations. It was reopened by His Worship the Mayor of Swindon, Councillor Ray Fisher on 23 April 2006.

The bandstand is an original feature of the gardens which were opened in 1894, but originally it had a weather vane instead of a clock.

In 1912 there was a benefit concert held here for the *Titanic* victims' families.

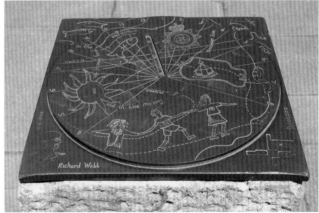

Above: *P.C. Webb memorial sundial in the Rose Garden in Old Town Gardens.*

Left: *The bandstand in Old Town Gardens.*

P.C. Webb Memorial Sundial (SU 152 835)

In the Rose Garden at Old Town Gardens stands a memorial sundial to P.C. Webb who died in 1988 after a battle with cancer. The sundial, which has now lost its gnomon, was installed in his memory in 1992 and funded by public subscription.

The brass sundial plate is engraved with the route of P.C. Webb's beat and tells the story of his courage in the face of his illness. He became the face of the hospital scanner campaign.

"K" Pillar Box Introduction (SU 125 838)

This needs no further explanation save to say that the commemoration is on the rear of the pillar box in Toothill's small precinct, near "The Watchers" artwork piece.

Teffont Magna

Golden Jubilee Sundial (ST 989 324)

Situated near the church in Teffont is a sundial erected to commemorate the Queen's Golden Jubilee. The plaque adequately describes the commemoration.

" This sundial commemorates the Golden Jubilee of Her Majesty Queen Elizabeth II, 2002."

Queen Elizabeth II Commemoration Stone
(ST 989 324)

There is a commemoration stone on a small green near the church in Teffont Magna. It is covered in lichen which makes it almost impossible to interpret. "Queen Elizabeth II," "1952" and "God Save the Queen" are legible.

I think the stone commemorates the accession to the throne of Queen Elizabeth II in 1952. However, renovating the stone would make it legible and correct my interpretation should it be wrong.

Teffont Magna Golden Jubilee Sundial.

Queen Elizabeth II Commemoration Stone.

Pitt Rivers Monument

Tollard Royal

Pitt Rivers Monument, Cranborne Chase
(ST 948 195)

This monument, a small tapered pillar, commemorates the excavation of a Romano-British village by Lieutenant General Pitt Rivers in 1886-7. The site is three quarters of a mile from the nearest road, which itself is a narrow lane. However, there is parking space available in the land adjacent to a road junction. It is reached by a public right of way south across fields. This a definite case of needing an ordnance survey map to locate the lane, footpath and monument site.

The monument is a tapered square column with three sides recording information about the finds and the fourth a dedication to Pitt Rivers. A series of pits and trenches still identify the location today. The excavations were probably filled in, but sinkage over time makes them appear partially filled in.

There were 15 skeletons found, 11 males and 4 females together with British and Roman coins and various relics of Roman origin. One of the column sides describes the average stature of the people determined from the skeletal remains – the men were 5ft 1.5 inches and the females were 4ft 10 inches tall. The remaining side has information about the skulls, but is difficult to decipher due to lichen.

Pitt Rivers was born in Yorkshire in 1827 as Augustus Henry Lane Fox. He changed his name to Pitt Rivers after inheriting the Cranborne Chase Estate from his great uncle in 1880. His career was in the army and served from 1845 until 1882, when he retired. During his time in the army he became interested in archaeology and amassed a large world-wide collection. He considered that all excavation should be supervised and detailed notes kept regarding even the smallest of finds and the strata from whence they came. He developed the idea of typology, which shows the developments of artefacts over time. His knowledge secured him the position of the first Inspector of Ancient Monuments in 1882.

The excavated finds from Cranborne Chase are in the Salisbury and South Wiltshire Museum. His other ethnographical finds from around the world are held in a museum in Oxford. His other claim to fame is as the creator of the Larmer Tree Gardens for public pleasure on the Rushmore Estate. They have been fully restored by his grandson Michael Pitt Rivers.

Trowbridge

Water Pump (ST 844 566)

The water pump on the road to Southwick stands in a façade for all the world like the frontage of a small church or chapel, but in fact is just the thickness of a

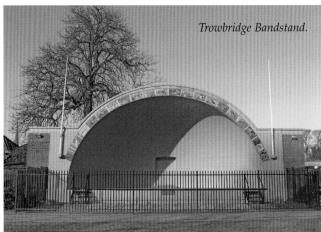

Trowbridge Bandstand.

1842 they took out a patent for apparatus for warming and ventilating buildings. It is for this activity they became known for advancements in the science of heating and ventilation.

There are metal railings separating the performers from the public, perhaps they are removed each time the stand is used. The railings were necessary because of vandalism and graffiti, which had become a serious problem before the stand was painted in 2014.

Tytherington

St James Church (ST 917 411)

A rather large information board placed on a green outside the church offers explanation with regard to its history. It reads in part:

"Founded prior to 1083. Church and a dwelling for two chaplains was endowed by the Empress Matilda, mother of King Henry II in 1140."

The original foundation date is mentioned as prior to 1083, but the present building according to the listing was founded in the twelfth century, being endowed by Matilda. The structure is Grade II* listed and has diminutive dimensions; 49ft X 13ft, but the walls are 3ft thick. It was restored in 1891 and has changed little since it was built. Of interest is that in 1820s there were but four services a year.

substantial recessed wall.

Inside the arched recess is a quotation from the bible: "Let him that at thirst come, and whosoever will let him take of the water of life freely."

Above the arch is a dedication in a recessed arched panel: "This well was given by the Reverend J. Hardman A.M. sometime incumbent of St. John's, Upper Studley, in memory of his beloved mother, Katherine Hardman, who died Jan. 15th 1860."

Reverend Hardman didn't live up to his name, as he must have thought a great deal of his mother! The well seems to be out of use.

Bandstand (ST 858 579)

The Trowbridge Bandstand is in Town Park and at the time of my photograph in January 2015 it appeared to be fully refurbished. There is a semi-circle of twenty blocks of mosaic tiles showing all manner of sporting activities with each block dedicated to a school in the area.

In the centre below the stage is a brass plate with a dedication reading:

"This bandstand was presented to his native town by William Nelson Haden in 1939 A.D. in memory of his forebears George Haden (1788 - 1856) and George Nelson Haden (1817 - 1892).

The Haden family are well known in Trowbridge as engineers. George Haden installed steam engines and maintained them for the woollen mills. He also took out patents for machinery – for dressing cloth in 1834 and manufacturing cloth in 1842. The company also became interested in heating and ventilating and in

Spotlight on Wattle, Daub and Window Tax

One may wonder what is the connection between wattle and daub and window tax. Well to be frank the only connection is that they are both terms used relative to housing. Wattle and daub is used in the construction of walls and window tax was a way of taxing homes, often resulting in blanked off windows obvious from the outside but thouroughly covered over within.

In Guilder Lane in Salisbury is a row of c. sixteenth century Grade II listed timber-framed cottages. On the upper floor of one of them is a glass fronted panel showing an unrendered wall section of infilling between the timbers, showing its structure. The Grade II listing explains this as lath and plaster infilling. A number of old oak framed properties in Wiltshire would have been constructed in this way, the Guilder Lane property serving as an example.

Above: *Not a window in the conventional sense, but a window showing the construction of the upper floor of the house, which is, between the timbers, made with wattle and daub.*

Left: *Cottages in Guilder Lane, Salisbury where some of the walls are constructed with wattle and daub.*

When this building was constructed such an infilling would have been known as wattle and daub. The wattle is composed of interwoven horizontal slats and vertical stathes. The stathes would have been fixed centrally to the surrounding timber frame with a combination of nails and location holes. The harder the timber (i.e. oak) the longer the timber would survive.

The daub component is composed of a binding agent, reinforcement and a filler. Typically a combination of some of the following: clay, dung, mud, sand, crushed stone, straw and hay. A pliable plug of hand worked daub with the chosen ingredients is pressed into the wattle to fill all voids, until a rough covering is made over both internal and external faces. The rough surface would have been lime plastered to give it protection and to achieve a smooth finish. Periodically a lime wash would have been applied to preserve the finish and protect the wall.

Window tax was introduced in 1696 under William III as a means of "Making good the deficiency of clipped money." It was common practice for criminals to clip money, in other words file or clip the edges of silver and gold coins. The filings and clippings were collected and melted down into ingots and sold to a gold or silversmith. The practice eventually stopped when the edges of coins were milled and worded (as our present one pound coin) together with, later, a change in the metal used which rendered the clipping of coins to be unprofitable.

Upon introduction of Window Tax, a flat rate of two shillings per house was imposed plus a variable rate of tax depending upon how many windows were present in the property above a base level of nine. Thus ten to nineteen windows had a total property levy of four shillings and above twenty windows the charge doubled to eight shillings. Various changes in how the tax was applied and system of charging were made over the time the tax was levied, including a lowering of the base level of windows upon which the tax started.

The tax was repealed in 1851 and was replaced with House Duty. The Government were forced to repeal the tax because campaigners argued that it was a tax on health, light and air. The term "daylight robbery" is often associated with the loss of light from blocked up windows and today we use the term for an unfair charge.

It was quite natural for house owners to desire a price reduction on their annual tax burden, so they blocked up windows to the threshold of tax application. New properties were being built with provision for extra windows, but were left bricked or stoned up, until the owner could afford extra tax or if the tax were to be changed or repealed. The blocking up of windows clearly reduced tax income for the government and this became clear when income had not increased over time, despite population growth and a corresponding increase in housing.

Blocked up windows are generally distributed throughout the county - some to the extent that false windows have been painted into blocked up spaces. Others have painted windows on walls merely to balance the appearance. Despite the repeal of the tax over 165 years ago there are a surprising number of window spaces that have never been opened and used for the purpose intended.

Left: A potential window facing the centre of Great Bedwyn village. Provision has been made for the sill and different toned brickwork for the framework of the window. Note the sun firemark in the centre of the prospective aperture.

Bottom left: A perfect example of a painted window in a window space. This is on the Grade II* listed Great Porch House in Devizes, which is included in the Devizes blue plaque heritage trail.

Bottom right: An example of a Wiltshire window that has been slabbed up with stone. I imagine the inside wall has long since been plastered and the need for the window is no longer paramount. The slabs appear to be of a different material to that used in the property construction, so there is every possibility this was at one time a glazed window, but the introduction of window tax caused it to be sealed up.

Upavon

Golden Jubilee Sarsen (SU 136 551)

In the centre of Upavon village stands a Golden Jubilee sarsen stone. There is a rather crudely displayed bronze plate which reads:

"To commemorate Queen Elizabeth II Golden Jubilee. 2nd June 2002." This plate, I feel, could have been better placed into a carved recess on the face of the stone.

Golden Jubilee Column (SU 131 548)

This, the second Queen Elizabeth II Golden Jubilee commemoration in Upavon, is a wooden column, probably oak, with a lion's head terminal. The wood has unfortunately split over time. The column has engraved a crown over EIIR, Golden Jubilee, 1952, a rose and 2002, in sequence from the column top to the base.

Left: *Upavon Jubilee Column.*

Right: *The John W. Hall Clock in Warminster.*

Warminster

John Hall Clock (ST 869 451)

This clock is associated with the Conservative Club of Warminster. There are two brass plaques on the wall beneath the clock which read:

"This memorial was unveiled by the Rt. Hon. Walter H. Long M.P. and presented on behalf of the memorial fund subscribers by the Warminster Tariff Reform League to the Conservative Club, Warminster."

"This clock is erected as a memorial of the life work of John W. Hall of this town, born 1830, died 1909. He was the pioneer of the Tariff Reform Movement in the West of England and he also played a leading part in its advocacy throughout the country consistently supporting it for nearly half a century. It is also a mark of the admiration and respect in which his memory is held by his numerous friends and fellow workers throughout the Empire. A.D. 1913."

The property upon which the clock is situated was once called Emwell House. Emwell was the name given to the High Cross that once stood in the position now occupied by the Obelisk. The clock seems to have moved with the headquarters of Warminster Conservative Club in the past, although the clock hasn't followed the Club to Prestbury Drive, the current headquarters.

The plaques both mention the Tariff Reform League, which was a pressure group formed in 1903 against foreign imports. They advocated support for British manufactured goods to protect British industry against foreign imports. I suspect the imports were cheaper – nothing changes!

The Warminster Obelisk on a road island.

Above: *The Silver Jubilee of Queen Elizabeth II is commemorated in Warminster's Lake Pleasure Gardens with a landscaping project and commemoration stone.*

Below: *Water Fountain in Lake Pleasure Gardens. Erected by William Frank Morgan.*

The Obelisk (ST 869 452)

The Obelisk stands in the middle of a small island triangle at the junction of Silver Street, Church Street and Vicarage Street. In the photograph of the Obelisk the John Hall Clock can be seen shortly after entering Church Street. It is a distinct feature in Warminster.

The Obelisk is a three sided tapering column topped with a reeded urn and a pineapple. It is Grade II* listed. It stands on the site of Warminster's medieval High Cross, known as Emwell Cross. There is a bronze plaque on the column which reads:

"The Obelisk. This Obelisk was constructed using surplus funds from the enclosure of the common lands of Warminster in 1783. The upkeep of the Obelisk is dedicated to the memory of Ken Rogers who once lived in, and loved, Warminster."

On the east corner of the Obelisk is a former drinking fountain with a lion's mask spout.

Silver Jubilee Commemoration (ST 875 448) and Water Fountain (ST 874 449)

Both the Warminster Silver Jubilee Commemoration Stone and the Memorial Water Fountain are in the Lake Pleasure Gardens.

To commemorate the Queen's Silver Jubilee in 1978 the Lake Pleasure Gardens were landscaped. The project was inaugurated by the Warminster Town Council and the finished project was dedicated on 30 April 1978. The scheme received a further award by the Council for the Protection of Rural England in the same year.

William Frank Morgan's name is over the door of the Maltings in Pound Street.

The Water Fountain is made from polished Aberdeen granite and formerly stood in the Market Place in Warminster. It was erected in 1892 by William Frank Morgan in memory of his wife Catherine. It is presently out of use.

William Frank Morgan was a maltster who owned Warminster Maltings. His name is over the door of the building in Pound Street. The Maltings were built in 1855 by his father William Morgan, who was already an established maltster in the town. In 1879 he handed down the business to his son, who in turn handed down the business to a relation, Edwin Sloper Beaven in 1902.

Queen Victoria Jubilee Plaque (ST 871 451)

This is both a work of art and a commemoration, but I include it as a commemoration because it celebrates the Golden Jubilee of Queen Victoria in 1897.

Around the outer segments of the large square central tile are the countries of Empire: Canada, Australia, New Zealand, Burmah (note spelling), Gibraltar, Malta, Cyprus, Egypt, Africa and West Indies. In the centre is the Queens head surrounded by the words Victoria 60 years Queen of Great Britain and Ireland, Empress of India.

This was the true age of Empire when Britain ruled the seas and swathed large parts of the world with the Union Jack. With two World Wars to follow and countries becoming independent of Britain, things have changed, but we do have a strong Commonwealth.

The Bath Arms (ST 875 451)

In the centre of Warminster town stands the Bath Arms. On the frontage of the building is a brass oval plaque, which is, unfortunately, difficult to read in sunlight due to strong reflections. The plaque gives a concise potted history of the building and I can do no better than quote from the plaque:

" This Grade II listed former coaching inn dates back to at least 1732 when the Three Goats' Heads' stood on the site and was let on the condition that it was rebuilt. The new inn was called The Kings Arms, but by 1769 was known as The Lords Arms, or Weymouth Arms after the Marquesses of Bath. Their lordships were also the Viscounts Weymouth, owners of the nearby Longleat Estate. By the early 1800s, the inn had become the Bath Arms Hotel.

These premises were refurbished by J.D. Wetherspoon in April 2014."

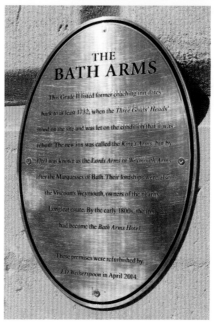

The Beyond Harvest statue is in The Cornmarket Mall in Warminster. When opened in 1990 the statue base had a small mouse, but this was stolen some time after.

Beyond Harvest (SU 876 451)

A blue plaque has been placed on a wall adjacent to the statue, which I quote: "This 1990 bronze sculpture by world renowned sculptor Colin Lambert, portrays a girl sitting on sacks of corn gazing towards Copheap and commemorates the days when Warminster was one of the West Country's foremost corn trading centres". Copheap is a small wooded hillock with a barrow to the north-east of the statue .

The girl on the corn sacks is supposed to be a likeness of Amy Flower who was an eighteen-year-old in the 1870s and came to the corn market from a farm at Chilmark with her brother.

Westbury

Matravers School Mosaic (ST 872 512)

A mosaic on the outside wall of a supermarket in Westbury was produced by the pupils of Matravers School to commemorate the links of the youth of Westbury with the youth of Chernobyl. The young

people of the Chernobyl region come to Westbury for holiday and respite.

The Chernobyl nuclear explosion in Ukraine on 26 April 1986 was the result of flawed reactor design operated by poorly trained personnel according to the World Nuclear Association. The steam explosion and fires released radioactive material into the atmosphere causing death and longer term cancers to people in the region. Ironically in 2011 Chernobyl was declared a tourist attraction!

West Lavington

Millennium Cross (SU 003 537)

The West Lavington Millennium Cross is situated in the entrance to Sandfields on a small green. On the tapered square base are dedications to the four churches in West Lavington together with other inscriptions. They read on the base chamfer:

"Dauntsey's Chapel. Ebeneezer Baptist Chapel. St. Joseph's Church. All Saints Church." On the tapered square sides they read:

"Erected 2000 A.D. by The Parish Council and the four parish churches. Mason and carved by the City of Bath College – stone masonry students. Designed by the pupils of Dauntsey's Aided Primary and Dauntsey's School. West (Bishop's) Lavington and Littleton Panell Millennium Cross."

There are carvings on all four sides of the tapered shaft. They depict farming and military activity on the Plain, a panel of tools, harvest, village property and other symbolic features.

West Lavington Millennium Cross.

Nigel Balchin (SU 005 533)

On a cottage in West Lavington High street is a circular plaque commemorating Nigel Balchin (1908 - 1970), who lived in the cottage while attending Dauntsey's School between 1919 and 1927. After leaving school he was trained in industrial psychology and assisted Roundtree's, in the capacity of consultant, to launch a number of iconic brands of chocolate.

Nigel Balchin first received acclaim as a novelist during the Second World War, when he wrote *Darkness Fall from the Air* in 1942. His other novels include *The Small Back Room* in 1943, which subsequently was made into a film in 1949 and *Kings of Infinite Space* in 1967.

He was also well known for writing screenplays, typically *Fame is the Spur* in 1947, *The Man Who Never Was* in 1955, for which he won the 1956 BAFTA award for Best British Screenplay and *The Singer not the Song* in 1961.

Nigel Balchin plaque in West Lavington High Street.

Wilton

Earl of Pembroke Statue (SU 101 312)

The statue stands on the entrance drive to Wilton House. It is of George Robert Charles Herbert 13th Earl of Pembroke and 10th Earl of Montgomery. On the plinth of the statue engraved in a panel is the *"Song Celestial"*, which was translated by Sir Edwin Arnold, poet and journalist.

George was born on 6 July 1850 and died 3 May 1895. The engraved plinth also records that the statue was placed in this position by his wife, his relations, neighbours and friends in loving recollection of his rare gifts of character and mind. He was succeeded by his younger brother Sydney.

He was a Conservative politician and became Under Secretary for War under Benjamin Disraeli between 1874 and 1875. He was also known as Lord Herbert of Lea between 1861 and 1862. His leisure time was spent as Master of Harriers then of foxhounds. One assumes this would have been the Wilton Hunt. After a riding accident his spare time was spent on the water, yachting.

Commemorative Seat (SU 101 314)

This stone seat is situated facing a recreation ground where bowls are played. There are two dedications on the seat, which is covered in lichen rendering it difficult to read. On the front face of the back rest are the following words:

"This ground is leased from the Earl of Pembroke to be used as a recreation ground for the inhabitants of Wilton.   September 1910. George Bell, Mayor." The mayor's surname is now very difficult to read. On the rear of the seat is another dedication:

"This stone is erected to commemorate the visit of King Edward VII to Wilton House, 27th June 1908, when near this spot His Majesty received an address of welcome from the Borough of Wilton, John M. Swayne, Mayor."

King Edward VII and Queen Alexandra arrived at Salisbury station by train, as one would expect at the beginning of the twentieth century – it was the fastest and most comfortable mode of transport. From the station they travelled through the streets of Salisbury to Wilton in a four-horse-drawn open coach. People lined the streets to welcome them. The following day they visited Longford Castle, no doubt again in the open top coach.

Queen Victoria's Diamond Jubilee (SU 096 312)

1897 was the year of Queen Victoria's Diamond Jubilee. Wilton chose to celebrate this with the erection of a church room of no particular architectural merit, which stands next to the magnificent Italianate church of St Mary and St Nicholas. The plaque shown is situated on the front wall of the building.

Queen Victoria's Diamond Jubilee in Wilton was celebrated with the construction of a church room.

The stone seat facing the bowling club in Wilton commemorates the visit of King Edward VII to Wilton House. Not the sort of seat most people would choose to sit on!

Marcus Aurelius (SU 099 311)

The bronze equestrian statue of Marcus Aurelius, Emperor of Rome between 161 and 180 AD, is surmounting the triumphal entrance arch to Wilton House. The statue is easily seen from the highway, from which this photograph was taken some years ago now, as it is presently partially covered during restoration work to the arch.

The arch was designed by Sir William Chambers in 1758 and originally erected on top of a hill to the south of the house. James Wyatt moved it to its present position in the nineteenth century.

The statue is a copy of that in the Musei Capitolini in Rome.

Wroughton

Cypher Wave (SU 161 793)

In the centre of the Alexandra Park development in Wroughton on a small green stands a sculpture by Jane Rickards called Cypher Wave. It stands on the site of the old Princess Alexandra RAF Hospital.

Jane Rickards, a local sculptor, won a competition to design and produce a sculpture to commemorate the heritage of this site. It was unveiled on 29 July 2006 and celebrated with a Hercules fly-past.

The sculpture has at its core a column of white flecked Kilkenny limestone standing as a monolith. Attached to the column are two steel wings, the whole forming a 12 ft. diameter circle.

The central monolith links the sculpture with the standing stones of the county, as in Stonehenge and Avebury and the wings provide the aeronautical link of the sculpture to the RAF and the site upon which it stands.

Wylye

Postilion Statue (SU 008 379)

The statue of a Postilion blowing his horn on a small island in the middle of the River Wylye is very difficult to see due to overhanging tree branches. The only view that I have been able to find is from the road bridge over the river. The statue is best seen in winter when the leaves have fallen. There is no access from the river bank.

The Postilion allegedly commemorates the drowning of the conductor of a stage coach in the first half of the eighteenth century, which crashed into the river when it was being forded. One assumes it was winter when the water was running fast and high.

The river was crossed by coaches, farm traffic and horses before 1750. Subsequently a bridge was built, probably when the road was turnpiked before 1773.

Cypher Wave on a small green in the centre of Alexandra Park housing development in Wroughton.

In the middle of the River Wylye can be seen the Postilion statue, best seen in winter.

Spotlight on White Horses and Other Hill Figures

Wiltshire is fortunate in having a large number of hill figures and emblems carved into the hillsides of the county. There is, of course, the fundamental requirement for a prominent hill figure to stand out in the landscape – an abundance of chalk. A large part of the county has chalk just below the turf. This is best seen when fields are tilled; the soil is tinted white with chalk pieces and undulations in the rural landscape show varying soil shadings depending upon how much chalk is in the soil structure.

On the hillsides the soil covering is thin and turf can be peeled away to show the white chalk beneath. When Iron Age man built hill forts for their security, the chalk excavations for banked and ditched enclosures on the tops of hills must have been visible for a great distance, until vegetation took over and blended the man-made features into the landscape. It would have been only a minor thought process that generated the idea of a tribal emblem cut into the chalk, to either welcome or warn others that this was their home.

Wiltshire has eight visible white horses and six lost figures in the county, as well as various military emblems. The military aspect of hill figures will be dealt with in another planned volume, which includes War and Remembrance. Much of the historical information regarding the county's hill figures originated with the published works of W.C. Plenderleath, who carried out intensive research in the latter part of the nineteenth century.

The oldest hill figure, the Uffington White Horse of Iron Age origin, is not in Wiltshire, but overlooks the White Horse Vale in Oxfordshire. However, it has always been associated with the Wiltshire horses being considered part of Wessex. Unfortunately none of the Wiltshire white horses are of known great age. Westbury has the distinction of being the oldest, dating from 1778, but this horse replaced an earlier naïve example, itself probably dating from the early eighteenth century. There are no records to suggest earlier dates on any of the hill figures lost or still visible. Having said this, the Uffington Horse is situated below an Iron Age hill fort and both Westbury and Cherhill are similarly situated. Who is to say that these camps did not have their own emblems now lost in time and overworked by more recent figures. I am sure the groups of people occupying their camps must have been aware of their neighbours' existence, albeit at some numbers of miles distant, perhaps they were known to them as "The White Horse Tribe".

With regard to the lost horses, the old Pewsey Horse, the lost figure at Roundway, Devizes and the early Westbury Horse are mentioned in the text for each of the extant horses at their respective locations. The others that are lost with no modern replacement or plans to reinstate them were at Ham Hill, Rockley and Tan Hill. The Ham Hill Horse was near the border with Berkshire. The vague outline of the Rockley Horse was not identified until 1949, but has since been put to the plough and lost. Records for the figure at Tan Hill are vague, but it has been referred to as a donkey, having been observed with a disproportionately large head.

The final lost figure is that of the Laverstock Panda. At dawn on 26 January 1969 a very large Panda head appeared on the hillside to the east of the village. For many years the Panda's appearance was a complete mystery. Eventually it was attributed to students at the University of North Wales. The rag week stunt involved a dozen recruits excavating the hill with spades following a grid pattern. They worked throughout darkness, perhaps, by moonlight, to cut a 55ft (16.8m) high work of hillside art. The Panda was cut again a year later, but soon fell into disrepair and only suggested features of the face remain, sufficient to make a positive location identification.

The Laverstock Panda.

In the description of extant white horse figures that follows, I have purposely avoided mentioning sizes for two reasons: In the first instance today's size and shape does not necessarily represent the originally designed horse's feature measurements at the time of first cutting the turf. Erosion, scouring and general maintenance will have altered both the shape and size over the years. Secondly, all the various sourced recorded dimensions have discrepancies, some significant. I have not considered making my own measurements, as some of the slopes on which the horses are cut are quite severe.

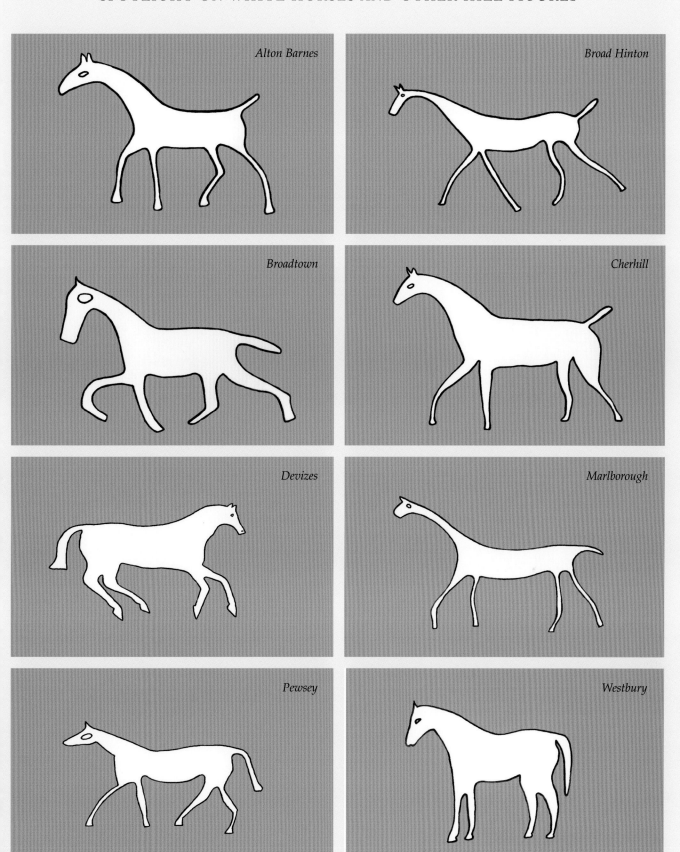

Alton Barnes

Broad Hinton

Broadtown

Cherhill

Devizes

Marlborough

Pewsey

Westbury

Needless to say all the figures are substantial in size so that they can be seen from some distance away. Some are proportionately greater in height than their living counterpart, for reasons of creating correct perspective from ground level. However to provide an idea of size I have averaged the length and height of all eight horses from dimensions that I believe are best probabilities giving dimensions of 108ft (32.9m) X 90ft (27.5m). I imagine that the Devizes Horse, being the most recent excavated, has accurate measurements: 150ft (45.7m) X 147ft (45m). This makes it one of the larger horses to grace the landscape of Wiltshire. The smallest horse is

The Laverstock Panda (top centre) is slowly being overtaken by nature. This view taken in the winter is the best time of year to pick out the fading features. The location is a view left from the road into Laverstock village from the A30 roundabout east of Salisbury. The ordnance survey grid reference of SU 1635 3175 is from the photograph observation point.

at Marlborough at about 62ft (18.9m) long and the largest is Westbury at approximately 180ft (54.8m).

Since the best perspective of each horse is either seen from an air approach or from ground level, depending on the intention of its designer, I have drawn each horse for comparison in shape with each other. The drawings are not to scale.

Alton Barnes White Horse (SU 107 637)

This prominent horse is a high stepping animal on the south side of Milk Hill, Alton Barnes. A well sited horse clearly visible from the highway between Alton Barnes and Devizes, but at certain vantage points can be seen from much further away.

The horse was cut in 1812 under the direction of farmer Mr Robert Pile. He paid £20 to Robert Thorne, who was better known in the area as a journeyman Jack the Painter, to design and cut his Alton Barnes Horse. He in turn sub-contracted the cutting of the turf and chalk compacting to John Harvey. It appears Jack the Painter was a rogue and absconded with the fee for the work without paying John Harvey a penny. Furthermore it seems the design may well have been copied from the Cherhill White Horse (1780) as there is a distinct similarity.

It is likely that John Harvey had already started work on the horse when Thorne absconded with the money. This would have substantially increased the cost of the horse as Robert Pile would have had to pay John Harvey. It is likely, in order to keep the cost to a

minimum, that Robert Pile would have played his part in finishing the horse.

This hill figure is kept well scoured. It received a substantial clean up by boy scouts and girl guides in 1935 for the Jubilee of King George V and Queen Mary, but would have been covered over in 1939 to prevent the enemy using it as a sighting beacon. It was completely renovated in 2010. It is said that the horse

The Alton Barnes Horse seen after harvest.

The sarsen boulder at Alton Priors.

Alton Barnes Horse detail sculpted into the sarsen.

can be seen from Old Sarum, Salisbury. I must confess not to have been able to see detail at a distance of some 22 miles, but then I have not considered the use of binoculars!

A short distance away from the village of Alton Barnes is the village of Alton Priors, a vantage point where the horse is clearly visible. On a small grass triangle at the entrance to the village from the main highway there is a lichen-covered sarsen stone (SU 111 623). The stone has an engraving of the Alton Barnes White Horse sculpted into the south face of the stone. It would benefit from scouring within the horse's shape before lichen obscures it. There is no indication of the artist that I could find on the stone.

Broad Hinton White Horse (SU 128 748)

The Broad Hinton White Horse is often referred to as the Hackpen Horse after the hill upon which it is situated. It lies on a gentle slope on the fringes of the Marlborough Downs to the right of the Broad Hinton to Marlborough road. The gentle slope of the hill gives the horse a foreshortened appearance making it look more like a fox than a horse. It has been scoured regularly by local villagers.

There seems little recorded history of the figure, with exception to its origin. It was cut by Henry Eatwell, parish clerk of Broad Hinton, and assisted by the local publican, Robert Witt, in 1838. The date suggests it was carved out of the hillside to celebrate the Coronation of Queen Victoria.

Broad Hinton or Hackpen Horse.

Broadtown White Horse (SU 099 783)

W.C. Plenderleath, the nineteenth century authority on white horses, believed the horse was cut by William Simmonds on the hillside on land of Littleton Farm in 1864. However, there is another record that suggests the horse was observed in 1863 and scoured at that time. Furthermore it was thought to be much older, probably dating from the early nineteenth century. Doubt is cast upon the story as the Broad Hinton Horse is only a few miles distant and confusion could have occurred between the two figures. In particular that the Broad Hinton Horse was already in existence in 1863, having been cut twenty-five years earlier.

In short Plenderleath's account seems more plausible. It is unlikely that if the Broadtown Horse was scoured in 1863 that further work would be necessary in 1864 by William Simmonds, assuming the possibility that he merely scoured an old horse and not created a new one.

The horse has a trotting stance and since 1991 has been maintained by Broadtown White Horse Restoration Society. It is best seen from Chapel Lane leading to the village from the Marlborough to Wootton Bassett road. It is on private land with no access to the public, with exception of the figure's maintenance.

Cherhill White Horse (SU 050 696)

The Cherhill Horse is the second oldest Wiltshire white horse, being cut in 1780, two years after the remodelling of the Westbury Horse, which may have been its inspiration. Dr Christopher Alsop of Calne created the figure on Cherhill Hill, east of Calne in a prominent position below Oldbury Fort earthwork. No doubt it was a significant landmark during coaching days on the road from London to Bath, not many miles after passing another landmark at Silbury Hill.

The Broadtown Horse with vegetation taking over the horse's legs.

The horse was carefully constructed to avoid perspective distortion. This was achieved by directing the marking out with a megaphone from some distance below and to the front of the horse. It was filled with compacted chalk with a number of upturned glass bottles to represent the eye. This would have caused the eye to glint on a sunny day and must have been seen from many miles away. Unfortunately the eye no longer contains glass, but consists of stones bound with concrete.

In 1935 it was scoured and renovated with a mixed spray of concrete and chalk slurry. By 2000 it had become very dilapidated again despite intermediate renovations and received major restoration in 2002. This involved refining the shape with shuttering to contain freshly applied compacted chalk. The work was financed with funds raised by the Cherhill White Horse Restoration Group. Cherhill Parish Council is now responsible for the upkeep of the horse.

The Cherhill Horse viewed almost at eye level. At tree level above the horse is Oldbury Iron Age Fort.

Right: *Detail of the horse's eye made with stones and concrete.*

Top: *The Devizes White Horse is the only chalk horse in Wiltshire to face right.* Above left: *Head detail of the Devizes Horse.* Above right: *Tail detail.*

Devizes White Horse (SU 016 641)

A letter to a local newspaper in 1998 from Sarah Padwick, a local resident, suggesting a chalk hill figure be cut on Roundway Down to celebrate the 2000 Millennium received an enthusiastic reception. A Devizes residents' committee was set up supported by Wiltshire Tourism to pursue the task.

Peter Greed, a member of the committee, designed the horse. In his youth he attended Devizes Grammar School, where, during the 1950s he made a detailed plan of an earlier horse cut by apprentice shoemakers in 1845 with a view to restoring it, but nothing came of the venture. The apprentices were referred to as "snobs", a name given to shoemakers in the nineteenth century. (My late father used this terminology when he was taking a pair of shoes to the local cobbler.)

Snobs Horse, as it was known, was cut in the vicinity of the Battle of Roundway fought on 13 July 1643 during the Civil War, when the Royalists decisively defeated the Roundheads. A second attempt at setting the wheels in motion to restore the old horse or cut a new one on the old site fell on deaf ears. The location was declared a site of scientific interest and Snobs

Horse could not be resurrected. I am not sure why the site was declared of scientific interest, but it was certainly historic.

It was fortuitous that a local farmer, Chris Combe, offered land on Roundway Hill, subject to permission from the landowner, The Crown Estate Commissioners. Permission, together with planning consent was granted and Peter Greed's design formed the basis of the new horse, which faces right, whereas all the other extant horses face left.

Funds to cut the horse were raised by public subscription with support from local organisations and schools. The marking out and outline cutting was carried out in August and September 1999. The final excavation and chalk compacting was carried out by Pearce Civil Engineering. On 1 January 2000 Devizes had a new white horse to grace Roundway Hill.

The white horse committee and members became known as "The Cavaliers of the Devizes Millennium White Horse", who ensured the continued maintenance and whitening of the figure. From 30 September 2011 the maintenance and care was handed over to Roundway Parish Council.

The horse is reached by taking the road to Roundway Hill from the London Road. The slope of the hill foreshortens the horse, but there is a gate to view the horse at close quarters.

Marlborough White Horse (SU 183 682)

The Marlborough White Horse should be more properly called the Preshute Horse as it is situated on Granham Hill above the village of Preshute. It is the smallest of Wiltshire's white horses and over the years its shape, through renovation, has become more stylised than a traditionally modelled horse; in fact to the extent of looking naïve.

It was created in 1804 by pupils of Marlborough Boys School, which was situated in the High Street and should not be confused with the later Marlborough College. Senior student William Canning sketched and pegged out the horse and together with fellow students carved out the shape and packed it with chalk. The head of the school was Mr Greasley, but upon his death in c. 1830 the school closed.

A new school opened in 1843 and later became a major English public school. Marlborough College as it is now known maintains the horse. Over the years it has been scoured and restored a number of times. In 1873, Captain Reed, who as a boy had taken part in the original cutting, scoured the horse. In 1935 it was restored by boy scouts for the Silver Jubilee of George V and Queen Mary. Another restoration took place after the war.

It is difficult to see at a distance in summer with surrounding trees in leaf, but there are glimpses from the Bath Road in front of Marlborough College, particularly in winter. It took me some time to actually find a close viewpoint. Travelling by car take the Bath Road west out of Marlborough and take the lane signposted to Manton, take the first left down Preshute Lane to the end of the lane. Here there is a car park for the church and a footpath that passes the rear of Marlborough College. On the right of the footpath after a short distance is a close view of the horse. The location can also be approached by walking from the opposite direction.

The Marlborough or Preshute White Horse. Note its slimline appearance, also the mounds at the end of the legs, which presumably are to prevent erosion giving it the appearance of a spider.

As with most of the hill figures they are best seen and photographed from the air, unfortunately I cannot fly! How good would it be to be a red kite and soar over the Wiltshire white horses and glance downward. Without the benefit of height I have chosen a distant viewpoint to try and correct perspective as much as I can. To achieve this a long telephoto lens is required to artificially bring the subject closer.

Such was the case with the Pewsey Horse shown here and that at Broad Hinton. The horses need regular scouring as grass soon invades the edges of the figures. The Pewsey Horse was beginning to lose its legs when I photographed it.

Pewsey White Horse (SU 171 580)

The Pewsey White Horse is on Pewsey Hill overlooking Pewsey Vale and about a mile south of Pewsey town. It can be reached from a minor road leading from the A345 Marlborough to Amesbury road.

The present horse replaced an earlier example situated close by, cut by Robert Pile in 1785, who later originated the Alton Barnes Horse. It fell into disrepair in the middle of the nineteenth century and eventually grassed over. The outline was still discernible before the First World War, but all trace has now disappeared, save for the fact that compacted chalk will still be present under the turf.

The impending coronation of George VI and Queen Elizabeth in 1937 instilled a desire in the community to celebrate the event with the cutting of a new horse. It is unclear why a new horse was scheduled to be excavated rather than restore the old one. George Marples of Sway, an authority on hill figures at the time designed three possibilities for the new horse, one of which had a rider in place. The final choice centred on the ease of keeping the figure in good trim; a well proportioned trotting horse. It is interesting to note that George Marples' son, Morris, wrote *White Horses and other Hill Figures* in 1949, which drew much from his father's work on the subject.

The 1937 horse was cut by Pewsey Fire Brigade.

George Marples added the date 1937 over the horse's back so that future generations would have no doubt regarding the date the horse was first cut into the hillside. Unfortunately the date has not been maintained and has disappeared. In common with all the chalk figures, the horse was camouflaged during the war to prevent it becoming a siting landmark for enemy aircraft. For this reason it was restored after the war by the Air Ministry.

It was scoured in 1985 by Pewsey firemen. Further restoration took place in 1998 and again in 2004. The Pewsey 6X Club, named after a local brew, presently keeps the horse in trim. It is fenced from grazing animals.

Westbury White Horse (ST 898 516)

The Westbury White Horse stands proudly on Bratton Down directly below the Iron Age hill fort of Bratton Camp; for this reason it is sometimes known as the Bratton White Horse. Bratton is associated with Alfred the Great and the Battle of Ethandun in 878, where Alfred decisively defeated the Danes. Ethandun is thought to be the modern day village of Edington, but a few miles away from Bratton Down.

There is no evidence to suggest that a horse was cut into the chalk at this site before the early eighteenth century, despite associations with Alfred's battle. However, who is to say that the Iron Age people occupying Bratton Camp did not have an emblem in chalk below the camp in common with Uffington, which overlooks the Vale of the White Horse east of Swindon. The present horse will have obscured any trace of Iron Age cutting.

The horse we see today, albeit with adjustments to its shape over the intervening years since it was cut into the chalk in 1778, is visible for miles to the west and is a well-known landmark travelling by train to the west through Westbury. It was cut under the direction of George Gee, steward to the landowner Lord Abingdon. Is it feasible that G. Gee was corrupted at the time the horse was cut or shortly after to gee-gee, the childish slang name we often call horses when talking to young children?

The present horse replaced an earlier example, probably cut between 1700 and 1760, which was smaller and more primitive looking, almost comical in appearance with short legs and bulbous eyes. The shape of the horse is known from an engraving dating from the 1760s, which shows the horse facing right. It is likely that the landowner did not like the strange appearance of the horse and instructed Mr Gee to arrange an improvement. The design of the 1778 horse was sufficient to obscure the older horse despite it facing in the opposite direction.

By 1850 the horse was in need of restoration and this was undertaken in 1853. The steepness of the slope caused erosion of the animal making it appear misshapen. Thus in 1873 an edging of stones was applied to maintain its shape. Concrete edging replaced the stones in 1936. Further work was carried out in the 1950s when the compacted chalk was replaced by concrete and the process was repeated in 1995. The concrete is now painted white giving the horse a striking appearance. It is cared for by English Heritage.

The Westbury White Horse can be seen from many miles distant.

Bibliography

Alderbury and Whaddon Local History Group. *More of the Mosaic of Alderbury and Whaddon*, 2011.
Bailey, Justin. *Lost Railways of Wiltshire*, Countryside Books, 2006.
Bergamar, Kate. *Discovering Hill Figures*, Shire Publications, 2008.
Cheetham, J.H. and Piper, John. *Wiltshire, A Shell Guide*, Faber and Faber, 1968 edition.
Chadwick, John C. *Wessex Peculiar – A Search for the Unusual*, Nigel J. Clark Publications.
Clew, Kenneth R. *The Kennet and Avon Canal*, David and Charles, 1985 edition.
Corfield, M.C. *A Guide to the Industrial Archaeology of Wiltshire*, Wiltshire County Council, 1978.
Daniels, Peter and Garraway Jones, Tim. *Salisbury Then and Now*, Tempus Publishing Ltd, 2003.
Delorme, Mary. *Curious Wiltshire*, Ex Libris Press, 1985.
Editorial Team. *The Sarum Chronicle*, the Hobnob Press annually.
Herbert, Jane. *We Wander in Wessex*, Ward Locke and Co. Ltd, 1947.
Hodge, Dr Bernulf. *A History of Malmesbury,*The friends of Malmesbury Abbey, 1968.
La Vardera, Dee. *The Little Book of Wiltshire*, The History Press, 2013.
Marples, Morris. *White Horses and Other Hill Figures*, Country Life Ltd, 1949.
Mee, Arthur. *The King's England – Wiltshire*, Hodder and Stoughton Ltd, 1939.
Olivier, Edith. *Wiltshire*, Robert Hale Ltd, 1951.
Pevsner, Nikolaus and Cherry, Bridget. *The Buildings of England - Wiltshire*, Penguin Books, 1999 ed.
Slocombe, Pamela M. *A Guide to the Industrial Archaeology of Wiltshire*, The Association for Industrial
    Archaeology, 2008.
Street, Pamela. *The Illustrated Portrait of Wiltshire*, Robert Hale Ltd, 1986 ed.
Watson, Michael. *Curiosities of Wiltshire*, S.B. Publications, 1994.
Waymouth, David. *Downton 7000 years of an English Village*, Downton Millennium Book Fund, 1999.
Whitlock, Ralph. *Wiltshire Folklore and Legends*, Robert Hale, 1992.
Whittock, Martyn. *Wiltshire Place Names*, Countryside Books, 1997.
Wiltshire Historic Churches Trust. *A Tour of Wiltshire Churches*, The Friary Press, undated.
Womens Institute. *Moonrakings – A Little Book of Wiltshire Stories*, 1979.
Wright, Geoffrey N. *Discovering Epitaphs*, Shire Publications Ltd, 1972.